About the author

Tony was born in Nottingham in 1952. In his twenties the seeds were sown for his love affair with Greece during a holiday on the island of Skiathos. Since then he has visited many of the islands of the Ionian and Aegean seas, as well as the mainland of Greece.

His heart though lies on the small-unspoilt islands of the Aegean. When in 2006 he had the opportunity of semi-retiring from his business consultancy, he and his partner Carol chose the island of Thassos as their base as UK ex-pats.

As an author of business books, Tony had been aware after his many years travelling within Greece that what was lacking for the holidaymaker and general traveller was a 'no holds barred' guide to the islands, with *all* the information that is required to have an exciting, informative and safe vacation brought together in one easy to read book.

In 2006 he wrote a book on his adopted island home of Thassos, which has become a benchmark for holiday guides, selling extensively in Europe and the United States.

And so, in 2007, after publishing his second book on Kos, he decided to write this latest book, on the island of Santorini. Tony hopes that in the years to come, his continuing travels will allow him to write guides for more of the Greek islands that he loves.

D1528985

Opposite: Wall fresco from the West House, ancient archaeological site of Akrotiri, circa 17th century B.C.

A-Z guide to

Santorini

Tony Oswin

Contents:
The island, its history, what to see, where to go, eating out,
entertainment, the best beaches, travel information and a host
of tips and hints for the holidaymaker and traveller.

2009 Edition

Tony Oswin

Published 2009 by arima publishing

www.arimapublishing.com

ISBN 978 1 84549 357 8

Printed and bound in the United Kingdom

Typeset in Arial 12/14

arima publishing
ASK House, Northgate Avenue
Bury St Edmunds, Suffolk IP32 6BB
t: (+44) 01284 700321

www.arimapublishing.com

To Carol Hart....for all her loving support

Foreword

I have been travelling to Greece for over thirty years and during that time I have fallen in love with the country, its people and most of all the Greek approach to life.

However, I realised many years ago, that one thing that was missing for the holidaymaker and visitor to the Greek islands, was a comprehensive publication written by someone who lives there, with *all* the necessary information and 'insider' knowledge, brought together in one easy to read book. Too many times, I have returned home from a visit to Greece, only to talk to someone who has advised me of something to do or see that I had had no knowledge of.

Hence this book. I hope you find it helpful and informative, not only during your stay, but when you are planning your holiday on Santorini.

Due to the wonders of modern publishing, the information contained within this book is updated on a regular basis and I would appreciate the readers' feedback by email to help in the revision and improvement of the information contained herewith. Through this, I aim to keep the book fresh, comprehensive and accurate.

For the latest information and news obtained mid-revision, you will find a 'Newsflash' page on the website detailed below.

I hope you have a wonderful visit to Santorini.

email: info@a-to-z-guide.co.uk

To view the other books in the 'A to Z' series visit

www.a-to-z-guide.co.uk

Contents

Santorini

'The spectacular island of Santorini'

Santorini (Greek - Σαντορίνη) is a small, circular archipelago of islands of volcanic origin, located in the southern Aegean Sea 110 kilometres north of the island of Crete and is the most southern of the Cyclades group of islands. In antiquety it was known as both Strongoli (the circular one) and Kallistē (the beautiful one), with the name of Santorini originating in the 13th century A.D., a derivative of Saint Irene. Herodotus (c.484 - c.425 B.C.), quotes the name of the island as being Thera in his book 'The Histories' and that is the official name it is known as today.

The island has an area of 73 sq km and a population of approximately 13,000. The island has no rivers, which means that water is scarce and until the late 20th century, the population collected rain water in cisterns, supplementing this with springwater and supplies imported from overseas. However, there is now a modern desalination plant that provides clean water to most areas.

Santorini is one of the most scenic islands of the Aegean. Whether during the day, when you can marvel at the moon-like landscapes, or by night, when both sunsets and moonsets can be viewed from exactly the same spot, you can't help but be enthralled.

Once a major exporter of pumice, the quarries were closed in 1986 to protect the volcanic caldera and now the primary industry is tourism, which in summer, significantly increases the resident population. Santorini's spectacular natural beauty and many attractions make it one of Greece's top tourist destinations.

Santorini can boast a small but successful wine industry, based on the grape variety Assyrtiko, which is resistant to Phylloxera (an insect related to the common aphid) that ravaged other European wine producing countries in the early 20th century. Assyrtiko vines are well adapted to the volcanic soils of Santorini, pruned to form low spiralling baskets, with the grapes protected inside the basket from chilling winds. The vines are widely planted, as their main source of water is nocturnal dew and sea mist. The white wines of Santorini are very dry, with a strong citrus scent and a slight sulphurous flavour, a result of the islands volcanic soils.

A traditional wine produced on the island is Vinsanto, which is a honey coloured white, sweet and an extremely strong dessert wine. The wine is made from sun-dried grapes and barrel-aged, which are both responsible for its colour and strength.

Santorini has its own international airport and is also a regular stop-off point for the many cruise liners that ply the Aegean.

The main settlements on Santorini are Fira, Oia (pronounced Eea), Emborio, Kamari. Imerovigli, Pyrgos and Thirassia.

Fira, the island's capital, is dramatically perched high on the cliffs overlooking the lagoon and at first glimpse, from your plane or ship, the whitewashed houses look like a scatter of sugar cubes on the cliff top.

The formation of the lagoon

Santorini was once a complete island with a typical volcanic peak. Then, many millennia ago, during the final throws of a major eruption, the subterranean roof of the emptied magma chamber collapsed, taking with it the both the flanks of the volcano and most of the island. This created a breach to the sea, which resulted in the flooding of the massively enlarged caldera, forming one of the largest on earth and creating the basic topography we see today.

During the following centuries, eruptions of the undersea volcanic vent, created an island within the caldera (similar to today's Nea Kameni). Apparently this then lay dormant until the late Bronze Age, as testified to by the frescoes found at Akrotiri, which clearly show the central island inhabited. It was then that this central volcano catastrophically erupted, and followed the same cycle of collapsing in on itself and disappearing under the lagoon.

Recent dendrochronological research*, ice-core findings in Greenland and radiocarbon dating, indicate that this eruption occurred between 1627 and 1600 B.C. These dates, however, conflict with the previous date range determined from the archaeological evidence, which placed the event between 1550 and 1500 B.C. My personal opinion is that the 1627 - 1600 date range will be the most accurate, but as the precise chronology is still in dispute, I shall henceforth just refer to the event as the 'Minoan eruption'.

The lagoon now measures 11 km by 7 km and is surrounded by cliffs that rise to 300 metres on three sides. The cliffs plunge spectacularly down to the lagoon, which at its deepest is almost 400 metres. On the fourth side of the island, the lagoon is separated from the Aegean by a much smaller island called Thirassia. This island is all that remains of the western flanks of the original volcano. The seaward flanks of the island on the north, east and southern sides slope down to the coastal agricultural areas.

All the island's ports are sited within the lagoon, as it provides safe harbour for even the largest liners.

The Minoan eruption

There is evidence of at least twelve major explosive eruptions in the last 200,000 years on Santorini. However, the Minoan eruption was one of the world's largest volcanic events in the last 10,000 years, estimated to have been ten times the magnitude of the Krakatoa eruption. About 30 cubic km (7 cubic miles) of magma and ash was ejected.

During the initial phase of the eruption, the plinian column rose to over 48 km (30 miles) into the stratosphere. The removal of such a large volume of magma eventually caused the volcano, centred in the middle of the ancient flooded caldera, to collapse in on itself and disappear under the lagoon. Ash fell over a large area of the eastern and southern Mediterranean. The collapse and subsequent explosion resulted in a catastrophic tsunami and the ash and gases released, caused major metrological and environmental damage throughout the eastern Mediterranean and in fact across the whole northern hemisphere. No trace of the islanders themselves has yet been found, but the present theory is that the pressures that this event placed on the Minoan civilisation as a whole, laid the seeds for its final collapse. It is interesting that around the time of the eruption, there was a fundamental change in Minoan art on Crete, from the glorification of athletics and the human form to what seems to be a fixation with all aspects of the sea and marine life. Was this a result of the psychological impact of both the eruption and the subsequent tsunami on the Minoans?

The many historical eruptions mean that the Santorini of today exhibits a complex stratification of overlapping 'shield volcano' layering. Basalt and andesite lava flows that make up the shields can be seen as banded layers in the cliff below the town of Fira. Whilst some of the cliff is thought to be a caldera wall associated with an eruption 21,000 year ago, the white layer at the top is the tephra (the air-borne material from an eruption) from the Minoan eruption.

After the Minoan eruption, there was a period of 1400 years, during which the volcano once again remained dormant. Then in 198

B.C., the volcano came alive, with an eruption centred in the middle of the lagoon, emanating from the volcanic vents below the sea, creating a new island called Hierra. Then in 46 A.D. a further eruption created another island, Theia. Finally, in 60 A.D. a third eruption united these two islands in to what is now called Palea Kameni (palea = old and Kameni = burnt). For the next 700 years the volcano lay dormant, then in 726, it once again erupted, increasing the size of Palea Kameni, with two further eruptions in 1457 and 1508 adding further material. The present height of the island is 110 metres above sea level.

In the 17th century eruptions in a new area of the lagoon created a further islet, then called Mikra Kameni (mikra means small). In 1707, further activity near Mikra created two new volcanic domes. They were called Aspronisi and Macronesi. Those were united in the course of the following five years by an island which formed between Palea and Mikra Kameni, much larger and higher than either and was called Nea Kameni (nea meaning new). This new island holds the distinction of being the youngest island in Greece.

The major volcanic eruptions since the Minoan event, date to 197 B.C., 1866, 1925 and 1949 -1950. The latter eruption on Nea Kameni was phreatic (explosive eruptions due to the hot magma coming in contact with water) and lasted less than a month. This eruption constructed a dome and produced lava flows. In 1956 Santorini suffered a major earthquake, although not followed by any volcanic activity, it caused severe damage on the island and resulted in the death of 49 people. Other volcanic vents on the archipelago include Akritiri, Thira, Skaros, Megalo Vouno, Mikro Profitis Ilias and Thirassia.

Santorini is renowned for the beautiful views from the villages situated on the cliffs of the lagoon and archipelago. These are especially magnificent at sunset. Tourists can visit the volcanic islands of Paleo and Nea Kameni by taking one of the daily cruises. Once on the shore of the larger island Nea Kameni, you can walk through the moon-like scenery and visit the volcano's crater and sulphuric steam vents.

Atlantis

I cannot of course complete this chapter without referring to the theory that Santorini was the setting for the fabled island of Atlantis. Whilst the debate continues, it is a fact that academics are renowned for being habitual sceptics. Only when a so-called 'outlandish' theory is proved correct, does everyone seem to jump on the bandwagon. It is then hard to find anyone who will admit that they initially ridiculed the theory in question!

I personally place more weight on the accuracy of both written and oral tradition and believe that the stories of Atlantis are like many others, based on the distant memory of a 'real' event.

One of the discoveries at the archaeological site at Akrotiri is a fresco, painted prior to the catastrophic eruption. This shows a representation of Santorini that bares a striking resemblance to the description of Atlantis as told in the account by Plato, written in circa. 375 B.C. Plato also described quarries on the island of Atlantis where "rocks of white, black, and red were extracted from the hills and used to construct a great island city". This description matches the composition of rocks found on Santorini.

The story Plato transcribed originated in Egypt, where it had been known for centuries. Evidence that Egypt was a trading partner of the Minoans (who were known by the Egyptians as the Keftiu), adds further credence to the truth of the theory.

The Minoan eruption occurred prior to detailed written records in the Minoan culture, but other eastern Mediterranean civilisations aside from the Egyptians, noted catastrophic events at this time. Results from Dendrochronology* on tree samples as far away as Ireland and California record adverse weather effects on tree growth and even more amazing, the Chinese recorded unusual climatic changes in the same period. Surely a natural disaster on *this scale* would find its way into 'oral tradition', so why is it so hard for some to believe in the story of Atlantis and that it was in fact based on the apocalyptic events on Santorini.

The 'Exodus' story

Recently, the Minoan eruption has also been linked by some scientists and theologists, to events portrayed in the biblical account of the exodus of the Hebrews out of Egypt. Certainly many of the so-called 'ten plagues of Egypt', have been recorded as occurring during and after other major volcanic eruptions. A further theory links the account of 'the parting of the Red Sea'** to the effects of a tsunami. As we have all seen in the pictures of the 'Boxing Day' tsunami, the sea initially rushes out from the coast, just prior to the tidal wave arriving.

This new evidence linked with the Minoan eruption has allowed some to postulate that prior to a resulting tsunami striking Egypt, there was a withdrawal of seawater from the coastal reed marshes. This could have made such areas temporarily passable to the Hebrews. The subsequent tidal wave however, would result in the devastation of anyone, or anything in the area. This would clearly make the story of the 'Exodus' more plausible.

However, the solid proof on either hypothesis is yet to be found and therefore the best that can be said is that 'the jury is out'.

* Dendrochronology or tree-ring dating, is the method of scientific dating, based on the analysis of tree-ring growth patterns. Changes in climatic conditions directly affect a trees growth pattern and therefore the size of its annual growth rings. These changes can be linked to such events as major volcanic eruptions and can be dated by cross-referencing a particular growth pattern to a 'library' of tree rings of known date.

** Recent research has confirmed, that the reference to the Red Sea in the story of the 'Exodus', is actually inaccurate and has resulted from a mis-translation from the original Hebrew texts. The correct translation refers to the 'Sea of Reeds'.

Tony Oswin

History

Prehistoric to classical period

According to the evidence found in Santorini's main archaeological sites, the first human presence on the island dates back to at least the Neolithic Period. Traces of settlement on the island found at Akrotiri date to around 3600 B.C. and confirm that the island was inhabited from the pre-Bronze Age.

Certainly the island was inhabited by either the Minoans, or a people with a very similar culture, as discoveries made at Akrotiri and Red Beach confirm. The evidence shows without doubt, that they were a highly sophisticated and cultured people. Their art is stylistically the same as that found on the island of Crete, such as Knossos, with many wall paintings and pottery showing naturalistic landscapes of animals and people in the same ancient Minoan style. However, the Minoan eruption seems to have brought to an end any habitation on the island, with no indication having been found of occupation during the following three centuries.

Evidence shows that around 1300 B.C., the Phoenicians settled on ancient Thira and stayed until about 1200 B.C. Then, around 1100 B.C., the island came under the control of the Lacedaemonians of mainland Greece, better known as the Spartans.

In the 9th century B.C., Dorians from north-western Greece (one of the four ancient Greek tribes) founded the main Hellenic city ('Ancient Thera') on the peak of Mesa Vouno, 400 metres above sea level. It is said that the city was named after their leader Theras.

A number of Dorian stone inscriptions have been found in the ruins of the city, especially in the vicinity of the Temple of Apollo, describing pederastic relationships within the community. Pederasty is a relationship between an adolescent boy and an adult male, who is not a direct family member. The intended aim at that time was that the adult (known as the 'erastes') would mentor and educate their 'eromenoi' (the ancient name for the boy) until manhood. However, many ancient scripts attest to these relationships being also homosexual in nature.

In ancient Sparta, young boys left their mother at the age of seven to join the 'agoge', the all-male institution, where the adolescents lived and underwent military training and moral teaching until the age of twenty.

In the 7th and 6th centuries B.C., Thira had commercial and trade relations with most of the islands and cities of Greece and founded cities elsewhere in the Mediterranean, such a Cyrene on the coast of Libya.

In the 5th century B.C., Dorian Thira refused to join the Delian League (a confederation of some Aegean city-states led by Athens, which was formed primarily to counter threats from the Persian Empire). Thira instead, allied itself with the opposing Peloponnesian League, led by Sparta. During the Peloponnesian War between the two leagues (431 - 404 B.C.), the Athenians took Thira and held it until the naval Battle of Aegospatami in 404 B.C., when the Spartans totally destroyed the Athenian fleet. The defeat resulted in Athens relinquishing its considerable economic and political influence in the Aegean to Sparta and the forced cessation of democracy in that city-state.

During the Hellenistic Period (323 - 27 B.C.), Thira, due to its strategic position in the Aegean, became an important trading centre and naval base for the ruling Ptolemies of Egypt. When Rome annexed Egypt, after the Battle of Actium (31 B.C.), between the forces of Octavian and those of Mark Antony and Cleopatra, Thira too was absorbed into the Roman Empire.

Under Rome and onwards

Under Roman domination Thira was initially used as an 'open prison' for dissidents exiled from Rome, but as the empire realised Thira's strategic importance, the island once again became an important trading centre in the Aegean.

In 330 A.D. when Emperor Constantine moved the centre of political power from Rome to Byzantium (Constantinople), Thira became part of the Byzantine Empire.

During the Christian Crusades (1095 - 1291 A.D.), the 'Franks' settled on the island making the fortress of Skaros their capital. Constant disputes between the different factions within the Franks, Turkish aggression, pirate raids and attempts by Byzantium to retake the island, meant that this period of the history of the island was one of conflict and upheaval.

In the 13th century, Thira was absorbed into the Duchy of Naxos. The duchy was created in 1207 by the Venetians as a way of increasing their influence and economic power in the Aegean. It was at this time that the island was renamed 'Santorini', after Saint Irene, a Christian martyr of the 3rd century A.D.

As political instability and piracy in the Aegean declined, the island again acquired it's own fleet and the economy improved.

In 1579, the island fell under Turkish occupation and became part of the Ottoman Empire. During this period the prosperity of the island continued to improve, confirmed by the fact that in 1821 the fleet of Santorini was the third largest in the Aegean, at 5,000 tons.

The island finally gained its independence in 1821 and joined the Greek Republic in 1830 after the signing of the London Protocol.

In 1939 at the beginning of the Second World War, Greece was invaded by Italy. However the Greek army routed the Italians and drove them back to the Albanian mountains. To save face and for strategic reasons, Germany as allies of Italy, diverted forces to aid the Italians and in 1940 the Axis forces defeated the Greek army and occupied the country. The Greeks suffered enormously under the German administration, both through starvation and severe restrictions. Later the Germans handed the administration over to their allies the Bulgarians, who's military and political authorities continued the severe treatment of the local population, until in November 1944 the Axis forces in Greece surrendered.

The Greek civil war (1946 -1949) posed as the first example of a post-war communist insurgency in Europe. The victory of the anti-communist government forces, led to Greece's membership in

NATO and helped to define the ideological balance of power in the Aegean during the 'Cold War'.

For those interested in history I have included a timeline of Greek and Roman events at the back of the book.

Mythology

Deucalion and Pyra

The story of Deucalion is a story similar to the biblical account of the flood. According to Greek mythology, Zeus, with the help of Poseidon (the god of the sea), decided to destroy humanity by flood, because he was tired of their sinful ways.

King Deucalion and his wife, Pyrrha, however, found favour with Poseidon and he arranged to spare them. Deucalion and Pyrrha were told in dreams to build a boat that would allow them to survive the imminent flood. After the deluge, they travelled in their boat until they came to a place called Parnassus, where they made sacrifices to Zeus. Zeus, upon seeing the sacrifices, sent Hermes the messenger god, to grant them whatever they wished for.

As the flood had destroyed all mankind, Deucalion and Pyrrha wished that they should not be left alone on Earth. Zeus hearing their request, ordered them both to cast stones onto the ground, the stones thrown by Deucalion became men, and those thrown by Pyrrha became women.

In the biblical story, Noah's sons become the 'founders' of specific racial identities; in the story of Deucalion the same theme is present. Deucalion and Pyrrha have two sons, Hellen and Amphictyon, and two daughters, Protogenia and Melantho. Hellen founded a town, Hellas, in Thessaly, whose inhabitants became known as the Graeci or Greeks, and later became known as the Hellenes.

Another similar ancient myth about a flood, relates to the angry reaction of Poseidon, when Athena defeated him in their rivalry over the domination of Athens. Poseidon in revenge flooded the whole of Attica.

These myths are chronologically placed to around the time of the Minoan eruption. It is therefore credible that these stories could be an attempt, by the people of that period; to explain the reason for the catastrophic tsunami that followed the eruption, in cultural and religion-based terms of the day.

Culture

For those who have not visited Greece before, how can I explain the Greek people and their culture? It could be said that their way of life reflects many of the positive attributes of the UK in the not so distant past. These include a greater reliance and respect within the community for the family as well as the individual, a belief that the quality of life is more important than the quantity and a stronger self-reliance, rather than an increasing dependence on the state.

All I will say is that I find the Greeks honest (especially on the islands), sincere and extremely friendly and one of my greatest hopes is that the ever-increasing exposure to the tourist trade does not devalue, or corrupt these virtues.

Many of the locals have two separate lives, the first during the holiday season, working in one of the many service industries dedicated to the tourist industry. Then once the tourists have left, another that is more reminiscent of the past life on the island, which includes amongst others agriculture, fishing and community services.

You will find that, as in many Mediterranean countries, much of the day-to-day activities start very early, then stop at lunchtime and reconvene early evening, continuing late into the night. So expect many of the shops and other services to be closed for a few hours in the afternoon. Remember the old adage 'only mad dogs and Englishmen go out in the midday sun. And by the way there are no mad dogs. You will see what seem like feral dogs wandering the streets, but most wear collars and are very friendly and lovable, if not entirely appreciated by the owners of the tavernas.

During your stay, one of the simplest ways of saying thank you (Efkaristo), is to take time to learn a few basic Greek words and phrases. I can assure you that even though the majority of the locals on Santorini speak at least a little English, it will be much appreciated by them. To that end, I have added a glossary of frequently used Greek words and phrases at the back of the book.

Beyond the tourist

With the first drops of rain another summer season comes to a close. The days get shorter and the sunsets are a deeper red and purple. The Meltemi winds (the Aegean equivalent of the French Mistral) appear even stronger in the evenings. There is a fresher feel in the air; reminding all on the island that the summer is over.

The warm sunny weather continues for the whole of September and into October. The first fallen leaves bring a new urgency, the tourists may be leaving but this is a busy time for the islanders, who return to many of the trades that have been replaced in the summer by tourism.

Only in mid-December can the people of Santorini slow down and start preparing for Christmas.

Winters on Santorini are mild, with temperatures dropping to around 10°C during January and February. Showers can be expected between October and May, with December tending to be the wettest month, rainfall is almost non-existent after March. The sun continues to shine during the winter, with Santorini still receiving roughly 4 to 5 hours a day during this time.

Cultural events

A number of culural events and festivals are staged by the islanders during the summer season. I have included the main events and a brief description of each.

Greek Easter does not always fall on the same date as that in most countries, as the Greek Orthodox Church uses the ancient Julian calendar, rather than the Gregorian calendar. In 2009 Easter Sunday falls on 19th April. Easter is the holiest of Greek holidays, and, as in other Christian traditions, it is also a celebration of spring.

During Easter in Greece, people leave the cities to spend the holiday in the countryside, usually in their ancestral villages.

Santorini is one of the very popular destinations for Greeks to spend a traditional Easter.

Food, of course, is central to the festivities, but not all Greeks eat the same Easter meal. The 'traditional' Easter fare varies regionally, although all over the country it mirrors the same age-old wisdom that nothing should be wasted.

Regional Greek Easter dishes include fresh herbs and tender young greens, dill, wild fennel, lemon balm, lettuce, sorrel and spinach. The meat chosen is usually lamb or goat; traditionally on Santorini it is goat.

One of the traditions of Greek Easter is to dye hard-boiled eggs red to signify the blood of Christ. At Easter, friends and family rap their egg against each other's, to see whose egg will survive un-cracked whilst saying in Greek, "Christ is risen" The other person says, "He is truly risen" This continues around the table until only one un-cracked egg is left. The owner of the egg being deemed lucky for the forthcoming year.

Epiphany

On the stroke of midnight on January 5th, the 'twelve days' of Christmas officially come to an end. However, the 6th, known as Epiphany, has a special significance in Greece and one of the age old ceremonies which takes place on this day, is the blessing of the sea and of the local boats.

The modern observance at Piraeus, the ancient port of Athens, takes the form of a priest hurling a large crucifix into the sea. Young men then brave the cold water and compete to retrieve it. These days, the cross is generally attached to a long chain, just in case that year's group of divers are less than proficient! After the diving, local fishermen bring their boats to be blessed by the priest.

The reason for the ceremony is that a tradition in the Greek Orthodox Church states that it was on this day that Christ was baptised by Saint John, and hence the connection with water.

On Epiphany, the Kallinkantzari (malicious spirits) who are said to be active during the twelve days of Christmas, are believed to be banished for the rest of the year.

Epiphany is also called the Phota or Fota, in reference to the day being a 'Feast of Light', and it is also the saint's day for Agia Theofana. While the biggest observance is at Piraeus, many islands and villages offer smaller versions of the event. It is definitely still a traditional holiday, performed by Greeks for Greeks.

The observance itself may pre-date Christianity. There was a ceremony around this date during the Roman period, to mark the opening of the maritime season. However, as any Greek fisherman will tell you, whatever the date of the opening of the maritime season really is, it definitely is not January 6th, as the inherent weather can still be stormy and uninviting.

The 6th is also said to be the approximate date of another festival held in the Roman period, during which emperors were worshiped. An ancient pagan festival was also held this time, when it was customary to give precious offerings to the sea, river and spring spirits to assure their benevolence.

Folklore and religious celebrations

Many religious events are continued, or have been revived, not only in respect for the history and religious beliefs of the islanders, but also as attractions for the tourists who visit Santorini.

Feast of Ipapandi	2nd Feb.	Finikia and Oia
Feast of Agios Epifanios	12th May	Akrotiri
Feast of Agios Theodosia	29th May	Fira
Feast of Agios Anargyros	1st July	Megalochori
Feast of the Prophet Ilias	20th July	Fira

Feast of Agios Ioannis	24th July	Monolithos
Epta Paidion	4th August	Oia
Feast of the Saviour's Metamorphosis	6th Aug.	Akrotiri
Feast of Koimiseos of Panagia	15th Aug.	Akrotiri
Feast of Panagia Episkopis (the major Saints' day)	15th Aug.	Episkopis Gonias
Feast of Dormation of the Virgin Mary	15th Aug.	Megalochori
Feast of Agios Ioannis	29th Aug.	Perissa
Feast of Panagia the Giatrissa	21st Sept.	Thirassia
Feast of Panagia Mirtidiotissa	24th Sept.	Kamari
Feast of Osios Averkios	22nd Oct.	Emborio

Most of the above are celebrations on the day of the particular church's patron saint. These often include open-air markets selling traditional products, food and wine.

The 'Ifaisteia' festival takes place in August and includes various cultural events, concerts, traditional dance performances and a 'volcanic' firework display.

The 'International Music Festival' is held in early September. Famous artists from all over the world perform at the Nomikos Conference Centre in Fira.

I advise that if you intend to visit one of these festivals, you check locally on the date, as these can often change.

Local products

Santorini has a fertile volcanic soil. Cultivated carefully over the years, this soil has made Santorini well known for its horticultural and viticultural products.

Grapes

On Santorini, the predominant grape variety is Assyrtiko that produces both a very dry white and a dessert appellation wine. The predominance on the island of volcanic ash, lava and pumice, has created the perfect soil conditions for the Assyrtiko vines and from these the very distinctive wines of Santorini. The main vineyards are situated near the village of Megalochori.

The island's vintners cultivate the vines in low 'basket' shaped crowns; the grapes are trained to grow within the 'baskets', to protect them from chilling winds. Due to the lack of water on the island, the vines obtain most of the water they need from the nocturnal sea mist and this, together with the fresh northerly winds, provides the excellent growing conditions for the grapes that make the superb Santorini wines.

The dessert wines from Santorini are called 'Vinsanto', a derivative of the name Santorini. Vinsanto can be naturally sweet, or fortified and must be barrel-aged for a minimum of two years. It is distinguished by its superb velvety palate with aromas of Crème Brûlée, chocolate and dried apricots.

Fava (split-peas)

Fava beans are grown on Santorini. Fava beans are a legume, smaller than a pea, but from the same family. They make superb dips and other appetizers, but they're also great in salads, sauces, sautés, stews, pastas and risottos. The island exports the beans to many countries around the world.

Tomatoes

A variety of tomato plant has been developed by the farmers on the island to cope with the lack of water. It produces tasty sweet cherry tomatoes that are both sold for eating and used in the manufacture of 'Belte', the famous concentrated tomato paste.

Katsouni

Katsouni is a type of cucumber, but is longer, thicker, a lighter colour and is sweeter than its better known cousin.

White eggplant (white aubergine)

White eggplant is a traditional crop of Santorini. The plant was originally introduced from Egypt during the period when pumice was exported to Suez for the construction of the canal. Due to the soil and climatic conditions, it is not bitter like other eggplants, being instead, sweet and juicy. Capers, courgettes and watermelon are also grown on Santorini.

Cheese

A brand of cheese called 'Chloro' is made from goat's milk that is dried and matured in brine. It is usually grated and used as an addition to food.

Pumice

Santorini used to export pumice stone, but as a measure to protect the caldera, the quarries were closed in 1986.

Crafts

Folk art

Weaving, painting and pottery are some of the many traditional folk arts to be found on the island. In the gift shops you will also find souvenirs made from pumice and the local volcanic stone.

Wine

As wine is such an important part of the economy on Santorini, it merits a special mention. The history of viticulture on the island goes back many millennia, as evidence found at the ancient site of Akrotiri confirms.

The uniqueness of Santorini wines comes from a number of factors, the volcanic soil, the micro-climate on the island and the varieties of grape grown. The area under cultivation is approximately 4,000 acres, however due to the low rainfall, the yield per acre is low. Total grape production lies between 1,500 and 4,500 tons, which translates into a wine production of between 1,050 and 3,150 tons per year.

There are 36 different varieties of grape grown on the island. However, only 4-5 varieties are represented in the main wine production.

The 'vintage' on Santorini takes place at the end of August and is a perfect time to visit the wineries.

White grape varieties

The most abundant variety used in white wine production is Assyrtiko, accounting for 80% of the total production. The variety produces a strong-bodied wine that has a high acidity with metallic characteristics.

A second variety is Athiri. This vine, of Cretan origin, is used with Assyrtiko grapes to create a style of white wine, which has a strong aroma.

The Aidani variety is used in the production of dessert wine Vinsanto to add aroma to the wine.

Red grape varieties

The variety of red grape known as Mavrotragona is indigenous to the island and is used in the manufacture of a rich red high alcoholic wine, which is high in tannins and of medium acidity.

Mantilaria produces a deep red coloured grape that consequently produces a rich bodied wine and medium alcoholic nature.

White wines

The most famous white wine on Santorini is Nykteri, derived from the Assyrtiko vine. The wine is barrel aged and has a characteristic metallic taste and high acidity.

Santorini is a fresh, dry white wine.

Assyrtiko wine, derived from the grape of the same name, is of high acidity and with a metallic element.

Vinsanto is a honey coloured sweet wine with a flavour of figs, raisins, and plums, made from grapes dried in the sun. There is also a Vinsanto sweet red wine.

Mezzo is a less sweet version of Vinsanto. The wine, which has a high acidity, has a flavour of peach and a lingering aftertaste of wildflower honey.

Red wines

Mavrathiro is a barrel aged sweet dark red wine.

Caldera is a dry red wine.

Brousko is a dry red, white or rosé wine.

Local animals

Donkeys

Horses, donkeys and mainly mules were the only means of transportation in Santorini up to the 1960's. They are part of the native charm and a symbol of Santorini. Today we can find them mainly at Gialos, the old port of Fira, where during the summer they carry tourists up and down the endless steep steps that connect Fira to the small port below. They are extremely adept at negotiating the steps, but beware, they do have a tendency to go fast!

Sheep and goats

Whilst sheep and goat rearing is not a major farming activity on Santorini, on your travels you will see large numbers (especially goats) in certain regions and it is obvious that the resulting meat and milk is an important addition to the islands food production.

Poultry

Free-range chickens are reared on the island and one thing I can say, having been used to factory-farmed varieties in the UK, is that they taste wonderful, especially when they are cooked on a rotisserie in the Greek way.

Dogs and cats

There are fewer cats on Santorini than most Greek islands, those there are, are outnumbered by the local dogs who wander free. However, the latter all seem to wear collars, so I presume they have owners. Whether part feral or owned, the dogs are very friendly and pose no problem, except that is for taverna staff who tend to chase them off for the sake of their diners.

Wild animals

For those interested in wildlife (the animal type), I have added the following information:

Apart from the odd feral goat and cat, wild mammals are scarce and inconspicuous on the island. Especially at night, the occasional brown rat can be seen scurrying across the road, or scavenging near to waste bins. At dusk, bats can be seen swooping through the evening sky feeding on the myriad of insects. The occasional dead hedgehog on the road, especially in the east, bares testament to their presence and in addition, stone martens and brown hares have also been seen on the island.

Greece reportedly supports ninety-five species of land mammals and research shows that Santorini shares in this diversity. Research has identified a distribution of twenty-five species of rodent around Greece. Just four species in total have been reported from the Aegean islands, namely the lesser mole rat, the broad-toothed field mouse, the brown rat and the house mouse.

Birds

There is a wide variety of bird life on the island (surprising as the locals shoot and trap them), including the common sparrow, finch, raven, crow, swift, martin, collared dove, lark, little owl, and an impressive range of birds of prey, which include kestrel, falcon, eagle, honey buzzard and sparrow-hawk. Marine birds include yellow-legged gulls, shearwaters and shags.

Dolphins

Although dolphins are to be found in the whole of the Mediterranean, they are a rare sight in open waters. However recently a pod was seen to 'play' in the bow wake of the ferries travelling to and from Santorini. So keep an eye out, you may just be lucky.

Tony Oswin

Getting there

Package holidays

The first and obvious way of visiting Santorini is by booking through a tour operator. The major UK companies that are offering holidays on Santorini in 2009 are in alphabetical order:-

Airtours	Olympic
Argo	Portland Direct
First Choice	Thomas Cook
Libra	Thomson (Tui)
Manos	

A la Carte

Most if not all of the major tour companies also offer flight-only alternatives and to give you an idea, the cost of a return flight from the UK into Santorini Airport during the summer season, start from around £120 per person. A small selection of flight only companies is listed below. I would advise however, that you search the web for the best deals for the dates you require.

http://www.charterflights.co.uk/

http://www.cheapflights.co.uk/

http://www.flydeals.co.uk

A second alternative is to fly by BA or Easyjet into Athens and then get a connecting flight to Santorini with Olympic or Aegean Airways. The flight time from Athens is about 30 mins. I won't quote costs as they vary dependant on time and date, but these can be found on the relevant websites.

The facilities at Santorini National Airport have recently been upgraded with new check-in-counters, conveyer belts, escalators and passenger facilities.

Santorini airport telephone number: +30 22860 28400

Hotels, studios and apartments

As you can appreciate there is a vast selection of holiday accommodation on the island, from pure luxury such as the Andronis Luxury Suites in Oia, boutique style hotels such as the Amerisa Suites in Fira, all the way down to a simple studio.

Whilst I could write a book just on accommodation, my advice would be to do your homework by obtaining a range of travel company brochures to decide on the resort and then search the web. As they say, one of the most important points is "location, location, location." If you want that quiet relaxing holiday, you don't want to be above a taverna and if you like the nightlife, you don't want to be in the middle of nowhere.

One point I believe is less important is for your accommodation to offer a restaurant service. One of the joys of Santorini, is to visit the vast choice of tavernas and restaurants on the island and enjoy what can invariably be attractive surroundings and good food. Who wants to frequent a hotel restaurant, when you can sit by the sea and watch the sun set over the caldera. If you have a family, you will find that the Greek culture is very family orientated and therefore children are welcomed and catered for by restaurant staff. Many tavernas offer breakfast, either continental or English.

One thing I can confirm is that without exception, the accommodation I have stayed in within Greece in the last 30 years has always been clean and good value for money. You may find that at the 'budget' end of the market, things can be a bit basic as far as room facilities are concerned. The top end of the market is as good as anything you will get back in the UK or US and for less!

Most apartments and studios will have at least a two-ring stove, a fridge and basic cutlery, pots and pans and utensils, a double or two single beds with side cupboards and a wardrobe (with never enough hangers). Usually there is only a shower (not a bath) with a W.C. For those who like a good nights sleep, it may be advisable if you are visiting in the high season, to select accommodation that has air-conditioning. Telephones and televisions in accommodation are usually to be found at the 'higher end' of the market.

One strange but positive anomaly I have noticed in the past, is that room cleaning and laundry changes occur more regularly than is specified in the brochure or room information. You should also find that when the odd problem such as a blocked sink or faulty light occurs, a quick talk with the management will invariably result in a quick resolution to the problem.

An alternative to booking before you leave home, is to take a flight to Santorini and look for your accommodation when you arrive on the island. You will find there is always some accommodation available and at most times you can negotiate a good price.

The days of locals putting out a 'vacancy' sign are all but over. If you arrive by boat you will likely be met by 'Kamakis', which means 'harpoon' (very fitting), who are touts that get paid by the hotels for each guest they introduce. In Fira, as with the other main resorts, there are a number of property companies and travel agencies who may have suitable accommodation on their books, or at least will point you in the right direction. Some of the agencies buy room space in advance (called commitment) to achieve better rates and therefore increase their income. It is therefore advisable to shop around, as some will offer bargain prices at certain times, since they would rather put you in a pre-paid room, than leave it empty and lose money.

Camping

For those who enjoy the 'back to nature' style holiday, or are looking for a 'budget' way of visiting Santorini, there are two campsites on the island. The sites are well laid out with shaded areas to set up your tent.

Santorini Camping

Contact: Giorgos Gioulis
Fira
84700
Santorini
Phone: +30 22860 22944 - 25062 - 63-64
Fax: +30 22860 25065
The site is 350 metres from the centre of Fira.

Facilities include:

24 hour hot water
Swimming pool
Pool bar
Mini-market
Self-service restaurant
Left luggage lockers and safe-deposit boxes
Kitchen facilities
Washing machine and ironing centre
Special sleeping bags areas
Rent a bed tent and rent a tent
Currency exchange, post and telephone services
Excursion booking
Wake up service
Free transfer from the port (high season)
Internet service

Perissa Camping

Contact: Galanakis Evagelos
Perissa
84703
Santorini
Phone: +30 22860 81343

Perissa Camping is located at Perissa beach.

Facilities include:

A taverna next to the beach
Beach bar
Mini-market
Left luggage lockers and safe-deposit boxes
Special sleeping bags areas
Rent a bed tent and rent a tent
Tourist office that provides: currency exchange, post and telephone services
Excursion booking
Free transfer from the port
Internet service

Tony Oswin

Places of interest

Places of interest on Santorini

Akrotiri

In the southwest peninsula of the island is the archaeological site of Akrotiri. However, due to a serious accident, the site has been closed to the public. I have endeavoured to obtain a date for a re-opening, but without success. Therefore, in the hope that the situation will change soon, I have included comprehensive details.

It was in the 1860's, that the remains of the ancient town were found by workmen quarrying volcanic ash for use in the construction of the Suez Canal. However, it wasn't until 1967 that academic excavations started at the site, under the direction of the late Professor Spyridon Marinatos. The professor died on the site after a fall and you can visit his grave, marked by flowers, by the side of one of the ancient walls near the exit.

The discoveries since 1967 have positioned Akrotiri as one of the most important archaeological sites in the Mediterranean. Only the southern tip of the large town has been uncovered, yet it has revealed complexes of buildings, streets and squares, with remains of walls standing as high as 8 metres, all entombed in the solidified ash deposited during the Minoan eruption.

The first habitation at the site dates from the Late Neolithic times (4th millennium B.C.). During the Early Bronze Age (3rd millennium B.C.), a sizeable settlement was founded and from the 20th to the 17th century B.C., the town developed into one of the main urban centres and ports in the Aegean. It is at this time that Santorini is believed to have become one of the most important trading partners of the Minoans, who were centred on Crete and may even have been one of their colonies.

The islanders cultivated olive trees and cereals, and reared a range of domesticated animals. They lived in highly advanced houses, many of three-storeys, some even with balconies. The town's design and infrastructure included innovations many centuries ahead of their time, such as an advanced drainage system.

The archaeological site

The area of excavation is large (200,000 square metres), but incredibly this is only approximately 4% of what is thought to remain of the town (see page 165). There are therefore decades of further excavation to undertake and work is ongoing on the site as the scaffolding and protective covers testify.

Entry is at the southern end of the site and if you walk up the paved ancient main-street, you will see on either side, the storerooms or warehouses of the ancient commercial city. During excavation in this area, a large number of Pithoi (large terracotta jars) were found and have been left in place. These still contained traces of olive oil, fish, and onions that were stored in the buildings. In approximately 100 metres, you will come to a vast area covered by a corrugated iron roof, erected to protect some of the most important finds from the elements. Information boards in four languages, including English, are located adjacent to all the main archaeological finds.

The wide variety of imported objects found in the buildings, indicate the considerable contact the islanders had with other cultures. There are artefacts from Crete, the Greek mainland, the Dodecanese, Cyprus, Syria and the animals portrayed in many of the frescoes such as antelope, monkeys, and wildcats confirm contact with Egypt and North Africa. Furthermore the discovery of a loom-workshop, suggests that textiles were one of the exports from the island.

Archaeological evidence seems to confirm that the town's life was terminated when the inhabitants were forced to abruptly abandon certainly the town, and possibly the island, as a result of severe earthquakes and seismic activity. This theory is reinforced by the fact that, as yet no remains have been found of the inhabitants of the town, as was the case with Pompeii. The indications that the inhabitants had prior warning, include personal possessions that have been piled up outside houses and beds that have been pulled out into the street. This though, also indicates that the warning was insufficient to give them time to vacate the town completely.

These earthquakes were the prelude to the major Minoan eruption, during which volcanic debris buried the town. This burial in ash and pumice has however, fortunately protected the buildings and their contents as well as, if not better, than at Pompeii.

The site was not a palace-complex such as those found on Crete, but its technologically advanced piped fresh water system, flushing 'toilets' (the latter being the oldest such 'convenience' discovered anywhere) and fine frescoes, confirm that this was not a conglomeration of low-status dwellings. The frescoes were originally removed to the National Archaeological Museum of Athens, for safekeeping. Some though have been returned and are displayed in the Prehistoric Thira Museum in the centre of Fira.

The frescoes discovered so far include amongst many scenes, one showing 'Saffron-Gatherers' offering their crocus-stamens to a seated lady, perhaps a goddess; another with two antelopes, painted with the kind of confident, flowing decorative style that one might expect in a Persian manuscript. There is also the famous fresco of a young fisherman with two bundles of fish strung by their gills (as shown on the title page of this book) and yet another depicting a flotilla of boats accompanied by leaping dolphins, with young women with parasols, relaxing in the boats.

One further example, representing a festival, illustrates two ports. The left port depicts members of the general population dressed in skins and tunics, a symbolic lion runs overhead. The right, probably of Akrotiri, shows a more aristocratic theme, with at its centre, a fleet of sailing ships at sea, with playful dolphins swimming alongside.

To get a true sense of the scale and urban complexity of this town, go to the plaza, near the exit, where you'll see two-storey buildings and a spacious open area. Imagine the scene 3,600 years ago of a bussling multi-cultural market place with islanders, traders and visitors from across the Mediterranean, going about their daily lives.

All of this and the many other marvels on the site, leave the visitor with a feeling of awe and incredulity that this was created by a civilisation so distant in time.

After the Minoan eruption, Santorini lay uninhabited for two centuries, whilst most likely, the peoples of the Aegean lost their fear of the island and the animal and plant life recovered.

Ancient Thira

The site of Ancient Thira is located on Mesa Vouno Mountain, at an altitude of 396 metres. Excavations began in 1895 and continued until 1903, directed by a German archaeologist, Baron Hiller Von Gartringen, who found many wonderful artefacts from the ancient city. The cemeteries on the northeast and northwest slopes were excavated by N. Zapheiropoulos from 1961 to 1982.

During its time, ancient Thira played host to Phoenicians, Dorians, Romans and Byzantines. Down the centre of the city runs the 'Sacred Way' and on either side are buildings that include groups of houses, market places, public baths, theatres, sanctuaries, the residence of Ptolemy Euergetes, tombs of the Archaic and Classical periods and early Christian churches. The ruins you see today are from the Hellenistic and Roman phases of the city.

The main monuments are:

Sanctuary of Artemidoros
Founded by Artemidoros of Perge, the sanctuary is entirely hewn from the rock and contains engraved epigrams and inscriptions including the symbols of the gods worshipped here. An eagle for Zeus, a lion for Apollo and a dolphin for Poseidon. Also engraved is the portrait of the wreathed Artemidoros, the founder of the sanctuary. The whole structure is dated to the late 4th or early 3rd century B.C.

Agora
The agora's southern precincts were the commercial heart of Thira, with the city's administration being conducted in what is now the central area. In the Roman period the northern precincts were added, which included a portico, monuments and sanctuaries erected in honour of dignitaries of the period.

Royal Stoa
The Royal Stoa is situated in the southwest of the part of the agora and measures 46 by 10 metres. The stoa dates from the reign of the Roman Emperor Augustus (27 B.C. - 14 A.D.) and consisted of

a colonnade of Doric pillars supporting a tiled roof, the main entry point was from the agora. In the northern section there were statues of members of Caesar's family and on the west wall, two inscribed slabs were added in 149 A.D. to record that the repairs to the portico were paid for by Kleitosthenes, a wealthy Theran.

Temple of Dionysos
Built in the 3rd century B.C., on an artificial terrace to the north of the Agora, this small Doric temple had a cella and pronaos. The facade and roof were constructed of marble, with local stone being employed for the remainder of the building.

Theatre
The theatre lies to the southeast of the Agora and was constructed in the Hellenistic period. In its original form it had a circular orchestra, however, during alterations in the 1st century A.D., the stage was extended, replacing part of the original orchestra.

Southeast of the city
This precinct were utilised exclusively for religious activities and contained sanctuaries, to Apollo Karneios, Hermes and Heracles. In the square, Gymnopaediae (dances of nude boys) were held in honour of Apollo Karneios. Engraved on the rocks are numerous inscriptions referring to both deities and youths dating from the Archaic to the Roman period. Near the Temple of Apollo are inscriptions that quote the names of men and boys who where involved in pederastic relationships (see page 13).

Sanctuary of Apollo Karneios
This 6th century B.C. sanctuary stands in part on an artificial terrace, with the remainder being hewn from the rock face. The temple comprises a pronaos and cella and a courtyard that comprises an underground cistern, the roof of which is supported by six large monolithic pillars. Next to the sanctuary is a small repository.

Gymnasium of the youths
Dated to the 2nd century A.D, this sanctuary to Hermes and Heracles is situated in a small cave, partially hewn from the rock.

Necropolis of ancient Thera

The necropolis (cemetery) is located on either side of the roads that led to the north and south harbours of the ancient city, the modern villages of Kamari and Perissa, respectively. The graves excavated span from the Archaic to the Roman periods.

The site of Ancient Thera is open Tuesday - Sunday: 8.30 a.m. - 3.00 p.m.

However, one word of warning, the road that leads up to the site from Kamari is not for the faint hearted, or those who suffer from vertigo. The road is cobbled and snakes its way up the mountain with many shear drops and no safety barriers.

Prehistoric Thira Museum

Located in Fira near the square, the Prehistoric Thira Museum is a must if you are interested in the history of the ancient town and island. Exhibits cover the period of inhabitation on Thira from Neolithic (New Stone Age) to the late Cycladic periods. Many amazing artefacts from ancient Akrotiri to 'day to day' items of the inhabitants are on show, including some of the beautiful frescoes found in the buildings.

Open 8:30 – 19:30, (closed Monday), entrance fee is 3 €.

Archaeological Museum

Located near the cable car in Fira town, the Archaeological Museum, is mainly dedicated to a collection of ceramics, including those known as 'Thira ware' and many Archaic and Classical pieces. There are though some Hellenistic and Roman sculptures and portraits. However, in my view the presentation of the exhibits is poor and many lack even descriptive labels.

Open 8:30 – 19:30, (closed Monday), entrance fee is 3 €.

Wine Museum

Situated in Vothonas on the road to Kamari beach, the wine museum presents the history of wine making on the island from 1660 to 1970. There are auto-guides and audio-visual effects and the visitor can watch the film 'The history of Santorini'. The museum is located in a natural cave 6 metres underground and 300 metres long.

The museum is open daily from 12:00 to 20:00 hrs.
Tel. (22860) 31322

Megaron Gyzi

Megaron Gyzi is a beautiful 17th century mansion-museum located in Fira. The museum is in the Halls of the Cultural Centre where the following six permanent exhibitions are located:-

- An exhibition of old Thiraic manucsripts, covering Santorini public life from the late 16th to the early 19th century.
- An exhibtion of engravings and maps from the 15th to the 19th century.
- A collection of paintings of Santorini donated by renouned Greek artists.
- A collection of paintings donated by Pintosacouple.
- A collection of photographs of Santorini covering the period between 1930 and 1956.
- A collection of Santorini strata.

Open between May 1st and October 31st.
Opening hours; 10:30 - 13:30 and 17:00 - 20:00.

Naval Museum

Situated in Oia, the Naval Museum is housed in an old mansion and portrays the maritime history of the island and its inhabitants. There are many exhibits that include rare figurheads, old maritime equipment and models of ancient and modern Thiran ships.

Open: 10:00 - 14:00 and 17:00 - 20:00 (closed Tuesday)

Folklore Museum

The folklore museum of Emmanoula A. Lignos is situated in Fira. This is a dwelling built in 1861 into a cave. The museum contains a host of exhibits which present the folklore of the island and the lives of the Thirans throughout history.

Open: 10:00 - 14:00 and 18:00 - 20:00

The Museum of Minerals and Fossils

Situated in the central square of Perissa, the museum has exhibits of minerals and fossils from both Santorini and further afield.

Winerys

Santorini is famous for its wine and therefore, whilst on the island, a visit to a winery should be on your itinery. Too many to mention in detail, I have included below a list of some of those open to the public:

Canava Roussos - Mesa Gonia, Kamari
Hatzidakis - Pyrgos Kallistis

Sigalas - between Foinikia and Baxedes

Argyros - Messa Gonia

Gavala - Megalochori

Gaia - on the road from Monolithos to Kamari

Antoniou - on the road from Fira to Megalochori

Koutsogiannopoulos - Vothonas

Associated Cooperative of Thiraic Products - Santo Wines - Pyrgos

Coach tours

If you prefer for someone else to 'take the strain', there are a number of guided bus tours that visit places of interest and attractions on the island. I would suggest you ask at the local travel agents, who will be able to advise you on the range and cost of the excursions available.

The Sea Diamond

On 5th April 2007 the cruise ship 'Sea Diamond' carrying 1,195 passengers, hit submerged rocks in the Caldera and sank early on the 6th. Sadly a French passenger and his daughter were unaccounted for and it is presumed that they went down with the ship. However, all other passengers and crew were rescued. She now lies bow up, between 62 and 180 metres down, directly below the Señor Zorba Mexican restaurant, 3 kms south of Fira town. There is a memorial plaque at the restaurant and you can see the inflatable skirt the authorities have put in place to trap the oil that is still leaking out of the ships fuel tanks.

Tony Oswin

Fira and the villages

The island's capital Fira, clings to the edge of a cliff that is, in fact, the rim of the ancient crater. The town is 300 metres above sea level and about 800 metres broad. If you arrive by ship there are winding steps that lead up to the town from the port below. You can either take a donkey up to the top, or as many prefer, the modern cable car.

The mule ride has however, been a tradition on Santorini for centuries, until the 1980's when the cable car was installed. The Swiss-made cable car, known as the 'Teleferique', was a gift from a wealthy Santorini ship owner called Nomikos, whose ships are regular visitors to the island. This made the journey up from the port for both tourists and their luggage less stressful. The mule owners did not lose out completely though, as they struck a deal to take a percentage of the revenue from the cable car (the cable car costs 4 € per ascent/descent).

Fira is a comparatively modern town, with houses built mostly during the 19th century, when the old Venetian capital at Skaros was abandoned due to earthquakes. The architecture is an attractive jumble of Venetian and Cycladic styles, one of the only similarities between the two being the whitewashed exteriors.

The impact of Aegean tourism has made itself felt in Fira, judging from the abundance of tavernas, hotels, discotheques and shops. It is the largest urban area on the island and acts as the central hub for the island's travel network and tourist facilities.

The town has a population of approximately 2,000 and it is a pleasure to stroll through the quaint and colourful cobbled streets, soaking up the charm of this pretty town and stopping for a coffee, or doing a bit of window-shopping for those souvenirs to take back home, but make sure you wear sensible shoes, the cobbles can reek havoc on the soles of your feet.

Looking toward the town of Oia from Fira you will see a large mountain. It has a path that leads to a couple of churches, which are popular as venues to make those wedding vows. It takes about an hour to reach the summit, but not a hike for the 'weak at heart'.

If you do decide to go, it could be an idea to go near sunset, as it is a popular place to watch the sunset. One tip though, make sure you take a flashlight for the return journey.

Santorini is essentially a beauty spot, an island whose cliffs seem to glow under the exceptionally clear light all day, but which at sunset glow red, evoking images of that catastrophic explosion more than 3,500 years ago. During the day the superb views from the cliff-edge overlook the two Kameni islands, the newest additions to the volcano, or better still, why not descend to the port and visit them by boat.

The villages (arranged in alphabetical order)

Akrotiri

Akrotiri village is situated on the furthest south-western peninsula of the island about 12 km from Fira. Excavations in the area discovered the town on the acropolis and a fortified Venetian castle, built during the medieval age, but destroyed after the occupation of Santorini by the Turks. There are two old churches in the village, Agia Triada and Ipapandi tou Sotiros.

Amoudi

Located below Oia it's a traditional Greek fishing village. The harbour offers an area for swimming and snorkeling, but there is no beach. However, if you walk around the rocky point past the tavernas, you will find small bay, which is good for sunbathing and the views are spectacular. Be cautious of swimming outside the cove, though, as currents can be very strong.

There are four tavernas, I suggest you try the fish here, it is so fresh and tasty. There is a bus service to Amoudi, that stops at Oia above; from there you either walk down the cliff path, or take a donkey ride.

Emborio

Emborio is a larger village with small picturesque streets and pretty whitewashed houses. The village also had a castle during the medieval age, remains of which are still visible. North of the village there is a strong, square fortified building named 'Goulas', in which the inhabitants sheltered during pirate raids.

Episkopi Gonias

Episkopi Gonias is located about 6 km from Fira near Kamari and has a pretty Byzantine church dedicated to the Assumption of the Virgin Mary. Built at the end of the 11th century, it was paid for by the Byzantine Emperor Alexios Komninos.

Finikia

This is a small village just outside Oia, which preserves many of the architectural and social elements of old Santorini. A lovely place to take a stroll and take in all the amazing colours and styles of the local houses.

Firostephani

Located north of Fira and really a continuance of the town, it also is perched on the edge of the cliffs. Once again from here you get stunning views of the caldera and volcano and there are a number of interesting churches to visit.

Imerovigli

Imerovigli is situated at the highest point on the rim of the caldera at over 300 metres above sea level. The village is a short distance from Fira and one of the villages that should not be missed during your vacation.

Beside the village is the castle of Scaros that guarded the western entrance to the island from attacks and its defences were never breached during its 600-year life. It was at the castle in 1207 that the Venetian leader Marko Sanouthos, after conquering the island, raised his Standard and renamed the island Santorini, after Saint Irene.

The village is well serviced by tavernas, restaurants, bars, shops, hotels and rooms to let.

Karterados

Only two kilometres from Fira, with interesting architecture and with the church of Analipsis, which is worth a visit.

Kodochori

An eastern superb of Fira it contains two beautiful mansions and a folklore museum.

Megalochori

The village of Megalochori is 6 km from Fira and contains the churches of Agia Anargyri, Isodia tis Theotokou and Agios Nikolaos Marmaritis on the road to Emborio, all worth a visit.

The church of Agios Nikolaos Marmaritis (Marmaro is the Greek name for marble), kept the Doric style of the 4th century B.C. temple previously situated on the site, when it was converted into a Christian church.

Messaria

Messaria is a very picturesque village, surrounded as it is by gardens and vineyards, situated 4 km from Fira in the centre of the island to the southeast.

As the prime location of wine production on the island, Messaria has recently seen the development of luxury hotels and specialist shops. The churches of Metamorphosis tou Sotiros and Agia Irini, both build between 1680 and 1700 and the church of Metropolis are all worth a visit.

Messaria has a Cycladic charm with its picturesque white washed houses and tiny winding streets. One of the most impressive buildings in the village is the Argiros Mansion, built in 1888 by winemaker George E. Argiros, seriously damaged by the 1956 earthquake, it has just recently been restored. It is a typical 19th century Santorini style home and if you are interested in architecture, it is worth a visit.

Messa Gonia

Messa Gonia is 9 km from Fira. The churches of Agia Anargyri, Isodia tis Theotokou and Agios Nikolaos Marmaritis on the road to Emborio are worth a visit.

Monolithos

Monolithos is a typical Santorini village, situated approximately 9 km from Fira and near the airport. Details of the beach of Monolithos can be found in a following chapter.

Oia

The traditional settlement of Oia is located on the northern tip of the island, high on the cliff-top, particularly popular with the honeymooners and couples as Oia hosts some of the most magnificent views on Santorini. Entered by a road, with cliffs on one side and sea on the other, the dramatic views add a further reason to visit this pretty and peaceful village.

The village square overlooks the sea and from here at sunset you can view and capture on your camera some fantastic sunset images. Ammoudi beach is directly below the village, accessible only by a steep path down the cliff.

The unique appeal of Oia lies in its village houses, many hewn out of the volcanic rock, with some whitewashed and others painted blue or ochre. There are also neo-classical mansions with their courtyards, narrow cobbled alleys and blue domes sparkling in the sunlight.

In 1900 the village had a population of close to 9,000. However, after the devastating earthquake of 1956 the population had dropped to just 500 permanent residents. The village has a strong maritime tradition and in 1951 Captain Antonis Dakoronia established a maritime museum in the village. Although like many other buildings, it was destroyed in 1956 earthquake, the museum reopened in 1979 and is open to visitors.

Oia has a cultural centre, an art gallery and a host of shops that sell handicrafts, jewellery, and a vast array of souvenirs.

Pyrgos

The village has some fine old houses, the remains of a Venetian castle on the hilltop (worthy only for the views from its 'battlements') and several Byzantine churches; the most notable is the Theotokaki, with some interesting frescoes.

The Monastery of Profitis Ilias, lies 3 km from the village. Located on the peak of the mountain of the same name, its construction started in 1771, with the help of the bishop of Fira, Zacharias, and the approval of the Patriarch of Constantinople (the Greek Orthodox equivalent of the Roman Catholic Pope).

After the Patriarch's spiritual protection for the monastery was pronounced, it was honoured by becoming a 'Patriarchical monastery'. In the 19th century the monastery was expanded from its original form, when the King of Greece, Othon, impressed by its charm, ordered further construction and embellishment.

The monastery's museum is full of ecclesiastical articles, including icons from 15th and 18th centuries, a 20th century iron cross, silver bound scriptures, and the diamond-adorned mitre of the Patriarch Gregory 5th.

The monastery plays host to a fascinating religious feast on 20th July each year.

Vothonas

The village of Vothonas is 6 km from the town of Fira. It is one the most picturesque villages on Santorini. You can usually be assured of peace and quiet to walk and enjoy this quaint village carved out of rocks. Vothonas village is the architectural showpiece of Santorini Island. There are many inspiring facades of houses that are conspicuous by their stylish doorways and pilasters that blend perfectly with the profusion of white domed houses.

A visit to Vothonas is incomplete without visiting the magnificent church of St. Anna, which happens to be the oldest church in the village, being built in 1827. The main focal point in the church is the intricately carved wooden panel, depicting scenes from the Old Testament.

Vourvoulos

Vourvoulos is a traditional village, located 2.5 km from Fira. Although the village is situated near to the capital, the beach of the same name is another 5 km from Fira on the northeast coast. There are good tavernas and cafés in the village as well as a bar and swimming pool.

Villages that are also beach resorts are covered in the next chapter.

Beaches

The two main beach resorts on the island are Kamari and Perissa, with Kamari being the most popular. A huge rocky outcrop separates the two beaches.

Below I have arranged all the main beaches in alphabetical order.

Ammoudi and Armeni

Ammoudi and Armeni are two beautiful beaches, which are the main beaches for those staying in Oia. The attractive town is built on the edge of the cliff above the beach. Ammoudi being directly below Oia, on the northwest tip of the island, while Armeni is a little further south.

Baxedes

Baxedes is the main beach at the northern end of the island. Located 3 km from the village of Oia, Baxedes is a quiet beach, with the usual black volcanic sand, ideal for those who like to avoid the 'hussle and bussle' of the more popular beaches. However, a drawback is that the beach can suffer when the Meltemi wind blows. The beach is serviced by a few tavernas.

Kamari

If it's a beach resort you are looking for on Santorini, then Kamari is the place for you. The black sandy beach, at least 8 km in length, is the main attraction of Kamari. On the seafront you will find hotels, restaurants, bars, discos and shops to please all tastes and budgets. In the day though, it can be quite sleepy and relaxed.

The town is connected by a frequent bus service to Fira. Completely rebuilt after the 1956 earthquake, Kamari was the most important strategic point on the island after the decline of Akrotiri in ancient times.

Not far from the village is the archaeological site of Ancient Thira. Also of potential interest in Kamari is the church of Panagia Episkopi, which was built in 1100 A.D. The best time to visit the church is on August 15th during the feast of the Virgin Mary, when the church celebrates with a large festival. You are invited to join in with the merry making, with plenty of food, dancing and singing taking place. If you are around on September 24th the church of Panagia Myrtidiotissa celebrates with a festival, where again the tourists are invited to dine and wine with the villages.

The beautiful black sandy beach of Kamari stretches for 8 km in length along the eastern coast of the island. You don't have to walk far to find taverns on the seafront as well as restaurants, hotels, tourist shops and entertainment spots. A number of water sports are also available like water skiing, windsurfing and paddleboats. There is a frequent bus service from Fira to Kamari.

Koloumbo

Koloumbo beach is next to Baxedes, the beach is mostly made up of white pebbles. If there is a strong wind, this is one beach to miss.

Monolithos

Just north of Kamari and on the eastern coast is the beach of Monolithos, most popular with the locals. Here you will find more peace and quiet than other Santorini beaches, but with all the facilities of the other beaches including a number of tavernas for drinks, snacks and meals.

Perissa

In the southern corner of the island is Perissa, known as another of the best beach resorts of Santorini. The beach is 7 km long and composed of black sand, this coupled with the clear deep blue sea create a stunning setting that attracts thousands of visitors every year. Seafront tavernas, hotels, camping facilities and trees for shade, add to the beach's popularity.

A number of hotels, restaurants, taverns, bars, discos and other facilities are available for the visitor. The beach offers one of the best water sports facilities on the island with windsurfing, water skiing and pedalos for hire.

The Byzantine church of Agia Irini (Saint Irene) is worth visiting and especially during August 29th and September 14th when festivals are held in honour of the patron saint of the island. Agia Irini died on the island while in exile in 304 A.D. Another attraction in the area is Ancient Thira, which is not far from Perissa.

Backpackers and the younger set seem to prefer Perissa Beach, which has the most affordable accommodation and facilities.

Perivolos

Perivolos is another of the quiet beaches on the island with small tavernas and studios and apartments to let directly behind the beach. Sports facilities are available on the beach, which is located on the southern tip of the island.

Red Beach

Not far from the ancient site at Akrotiri, is Red Beach (also known as Kokini Paralia). You couldn't ask for a more breathtaking setting for a swim. Soaring red lava cliffs that form a backdrop to the black sandy shore, with a clear turquoise sea, all add to the very picturesque setting for that day on the beach. The nearby hotel can be the venue for that lazy lunch and if you like excursions, boats leave from Akrotiri to other beaches further down the southwest coast.

Vlihada

Situated at the southwest end of the island, 13 km from Fira, Vlihada is a very beautiful quiet beach and is a perfect spot for those wishing to avoid the big crowds.

The long beach is composed of the usual volcanic sands and is sheltered by the cliffs behind. These have been eroded by the wind and sea to form small caves and an overall moon-like landscape, which adds to the strange but scenic attraction of this beach.

Vourvoulos

Vourvoulos beach is a mere 7 km from Fira, located on the northeast coastline. The beach is sandy with a turquoise blue sea and in the right conditions; it is ideal for swimming and sun bathing. The plus of Vourvoulos beach is that it is among the lesser-known beaches of Santorini and therefore you can achieve some privacy and peace.

Regrettably though, the beach is not as well maintained as others on the island and can be a little litter strewn. Also, when the Meltemi blows, sunbathing can be unpleasant and the seas can become very rough. In these conditions it is advisable when swimming, not to stray too far from the shoreline.

Activities

Organised trips

Most tour companies will offer a range of excursions to their customers at the traditional 'welcome meeting'. These range from the sometimes-abused title of a 'Greek Night', day boat trips around the caldera including a barbeque, spa days, to trips to the local winerys.

Many of the excursions can also be found independently, through the many tour companies situated in the towns on the island. Whilst the choice is down to the individual, before booking with your tour operator, I would recommend you shop around to see what offers are available and if possible talk to other holidaymakers who have already been on the tour in question.

Activities for the very young

If you have booked hotel accommodation through a tour company, most offer activities for the very young within the hotel precincts, these should be listed in the company's brochure.

Other than the obvious days on the beach, I will outline a range of activities that are suitable for children.

In or near some of the main resorts you can usually find a limited number of fairground attractions for an evening treat including dodgem rides, toy train rides and mini-carousels.

Boat trips can be booked in most resorts, as can pedalo hire, banana rides and paragliding. The horse riding stables on the island also offer pony rides for the young, ask locally which is the nearest.

Most of the larger supermarkets and souvenir shops stock a wide range of toys, including such things as childrens' fishing kits, snorkelling sets and fun beach items, such as bucket and spades, lilos, toy dinghies, frisbees, beach balls, racket ball sets, etc.

Pubs, bars and adrenalin

Due to its size and diversity, Santorini lacks the all-out day party scene of Mykonos or Kos. However, being the third most popular and tourist-island of the Dodecanese after Rhodes and Kos, Santorini has a vast selection of nightlife.

Most of the lively bars and nightclubs of Santorini are concentrated in Fira, it is the prime gathering spot on the island, the place where people begin and often end their nights. Dress codes do apply in some clubs. Many of the clubs and bars along the caldera cliff are renovated 'cave houses'.

Clubs tend to be indoors or surrounded by high walls due to the strict noise abatement laws, whereas many of the bars, as they close earlier, can offer beautiful views of the caldera from their patios.

True to my word of being unbiased and independent, I will not comment on which is best or worst. The bars and clubs also cater for different tastes and therefore one seen as cool by one person, could be totally un-cool to others.

To give you a flavour of the nightlife, I have outlined below a selection of the main venues and their facilities. My suggestion though, is to talk to the locals and those tourists who have already sampled what's on and make your own decision.

Bars

Fira and the other main resorts are bursting with bars and pubs and there's something to suit everyone. From the latest dance anthems to the cheesiest tunes, a great indie scene and a splash of funky house and R'n'B, the music is non-stop and the bars can get packed with revellers. Music is usually played until midnight, when if you still have the energy, the clubs take over.

Tropical Bar is a sophisticated euro tunes venue. With a wide bar counter (ideal for dancing) and a balcony with a spectacular view of the caldera. Friendly and social, it makes a great venue to start the night off as you mean to go on.

The Two Brothers Bar in Fira is a very lively bar. The brothers are generous with the shots, the DJ knows how to keep the joint jumping and it's fun. It's somewhat hidden, just past the main part of town down an alley. Look for the sign over door.

Kastro Cafeteria, is located at the cable car entrance and offers both the facilities of a bar and taverna, with a great view of the volcano. The cool breeze and the comfy chairs are the perfect companion to parched throats and tired feet.

Other bars include: music style

Fira:

Art Café

Bar 33   - Greek

Café Del Mar

Casablanca   - soul

Classico café   - background

Ellenes   - Greek

Francos Bar   - classical

Kira Thira Bar   - jazz/rock

Lava Café

Murphy's Bar   - mainstream

Remvi

Select Café — international

Tango Bar — mainstream

Tithora

Kamari:

Ethnic Café bar — ethnic/rock

Hook Bar — rock

Mango Bar — mainstream

Valentino's — sophisticated

Yellow Donkey Disco

Katrados:

Mojito Café — background

Oia:

Bar 1800 — sophisticated

Oias Café Gallery

Papagalos Café

Pelekanos Café — atmospheric

Zorbas

Perissa:

Yazz Beach Bar   - mainsteam

Perivolos:

Salty Beach Club

Wet Beach Bar   - mainstream

Privolos:

Chilli Beach Bar

Many people gather in Oia to watch the sunset. If you are then off to party in Fira, the Tropical Bar offers some spectacular views while you enjoy that early evening cocktail.

Clubs

As good as the bar-life is, if you want to go clubbing, holidays on Santorini will still live up to all your expectations. Bars are mostly free, but the clubs charge around 3 - 10 € entrance fee. Prices for drinks at the venues around the towns are quite reasonable, probably the same if not a little cheaper than back in the UK or US. The club opening hours are:-

Sunday to Thursday - 12 midnight - 4am
Friday and Saturday - 12 midnight - 6am

Koo club is Santorini's most established club and the most famous night venue on Santorini. It is always crowded with revellers in a mood to dance and party, a testament to its popularity among tourists, locals and European celebrities.

It has a large outdoor patio in a tropical setting in contrast to the high-energy dance scene inside.

Enigma club was established in the summer of 1979. A large club with a great atmosphere and decorated with imposing arches, mood lighting, cushioned benches and a great dance scene. Outside there is a large seating area, ideal for relaxing between dances.

Dom club is one of the liveliest nightclubs and it is located in Kamari. With a 'cage' on stage, the non-stop partying goes on until the very early hours.

Other clubs include:

Casablanca Soul	- Fira
Club 33	- Fira
Mamounia	- Fira
Town	- Fira

During the day, beach bars can be a great venue if you want sun bathing with a 'little extra'.

Adrenalin

There's so much to do and yet days can be as chilled out or action-filled as you like. For adrenalin junkies don't miss the speedboat trips and loads of other exhilarating water and land-based activities. For the more laid back, relax and catch some rays, or check out the volcanic islands in the lagoon.

Or how about a Jeep safari, you will find these advertised in the local tour company offices.

Dependant on the company, they either pick you up at your hotel, or from a convenient collection point. You will travel in a convoy of jeeps following an experienced guide over mountains, through volcanic landscapes and down dirt tracks to the coast. This is a great day out, taking in the lovely landscape of Santorini and its villages.

Lunch is organised along the route at either a taverna, or alternatively, a picnic or BBQ on the beach.

One word of warning though, take plenty of sun-tan oil and some good protective clothing, with the jeeps being open to the sun, you can come back looking like a lobster……oh and one more thing, don't forget the driving licence!

Visiting the Volcano

I have added this activity under 'Adrenalin' as to be honest you will need a good supply to complete this trip. In my view though, to stand on the summit of a live volcano and take in the incredible moon-like landscape all around, the expenditure is well worth it.

These tours are offered by a cooperative of boat operators called the 'Ships Joint Venture of Santorini'. There are 8 tours to choose from, ranging from a simple boat trip to the volcano, to a combined boat and coach tour which takes in the volcano, Thirassia and sunset at Oia. I have outlined their tour 2 on the next page.

The tours can be booked at most of the travel agents in the towns and resorts. Tour 2 starts at 11:00 and 14:00 and departs from the Old Port below Fira. The cost is 18 € per person.

A traditional Caicque takes you first out to Nea Kameni, the youngest and still active (but at present dormant) volcano. You land on the island and take a well-worn path past a number of previously active craters, finally reaching the summit and the latest addition to the list of volcanic vents.

Returning to the boat, it then moves on to Palea Kameni, where it drops anchor for those who would like to swim in the hot mineral springs that emanate from deep underground on this island.

The boat then returns to the Old Port, the round trip takes about 3 hours.

If you book one of these tours and I do recommend them, then I would advise you to wear sturdy walking shoes, apply a high-factor sun cream, take plenty of fluids and a good hat. I know this will sound a bit excessive, but also add an umbrella, you will in the end I am sure find it invaluable. In the height of summer the volcano bakes (having no vegetation) and the heat seems to hit you from all directions. Whilst there are shaded seating areas along the route, these are small, so it is in my view better to take your shade with you!

One last point, if you are a good swimmer and would like to take advantage of the swim off the boat at Palea Kameni, remember to take a towel as these are not provided. The swimming stop lasts for about an hour, with those not participating staying on board.

Sports and recreation

Fishing

Fishing is a popular pastime on the island for the locals, both by boat and off-shore, but for those visitors who would like to relax and try their luck with a rod and tackle, then most of the main resorts have a shop selling fishing tackle and bait.

It is often the local hardware retailer or similar, that doubles up as a fishing shop and although I am not an experienced fisherman, I have been surprised at the quality and range of gear on offer and the low cost of the items. To give an idea to the interested reader, a good extendable rod is around 20 €.

The sea around the island abounds with a wide variety of fish, a fact that confirms the absence of pollution. The species include mullet, bream, blackfish, grey pandora, picarel and horse mackerel, with molluscs and crustaceans such as octopus and lobster.

Boat hire

Small outboard boats such as RIB boats can be hired from some of the beaches on an hr/day basis. Larger sea going boats can be hired on the island on a daily or weekly basis.

Paragliding

There is paragliding on most major beaches.

Jet skis

Jet skis are available for hire on a number of beaches.

Banana boats and ringos

For those not conversant with this activity, a banana boat is a long thin inflatable with seats for the participants positioned down its length. The 'banana' is towed behind a speedboat and the objective is to stay on and enjoy the ride. Ringos are an alternative to the banana and are large inflatable rings towed behind the boat.

Banana and/or ringo rides can be found at all the main beaches. For safety's sake it is important that you wear the life jacket supplied.

Windsurfing

Windsurfing is available on many of the larger beaches.

Sub-aqua

To my knowledge there are only three certified dive-centres on Santorini, namely the Volcano Diving Centre at Kamari beach, the Mediterranean Dive Club at Perissa and the Santorini Dive Centre, which is also at Perissa.

Cycling

There are a number of cycle hire shops on the island, so I suggest you ask at your hotel/apartments, they should be able to give you directions to the nearest. Bike hire charges range from 4 to 12 € a day, cheaper if you hire for several days. Cycles come with locks so you needn't worry about security, but beware, they all look the same, so it's a good idea to tie something on it, so you can spot which one is yours. One other tip is don't try to load a bike onto a local bus, they are not allowed.

Spa and fitness

There are a number of the larger hotels on the island that have spas and gyms that are open to non-residents and one independent spa centre in Fira. My advice would be to ask locally where the nearest facilities are and check beforehand their availability and price.

Cinemas

Although not a sport, I have added the cinemas here as a further entertainment for the visitor. As we are in Greece it is always advisable to check the times before going. There are three cinemas on Santorini:-

The Cinetheatre, Fira - Is an open-air cinema, with a bar for snacks and refreshments.
Films start every evening at 21:00 and 23:15
Films are shown in original versions with Greek sub-titles.
Open during summer season, tel : 28881

Cine Villaggio, Kamari - An indoor cinema with air conditioning. snack bar and refreshments.
Films start every evening at 19:30 and 22:30
Films are shown in original versions with Greek sub-titles.
Open all year round - tel : 32800

Open Air Cinema - As the name implies it is open-air. Situated on the road to Kamari.
Films start every evening at 21:00 and 23:15
Films are shown in original versions with Greek sub-titles.
Open during the summer months June - September, tel : 31974

Tennis, mini-golf, etc.

There are a vast array of other activities of the island, too many to mention here, such as tennis and mini-golf. My advice would be therefore to ask locally what is available and the quality of the venue.

Donkey rides

On the cliff in Fira, is a set of steps leading to the cruise ship port. Donkey rides are available from the top to the bottom and vice versa. I would suggest you walk down and take a donkey ride back. But beware were you are treading; the donkeys do tend to leave their mark!

Tony Oswin

Getting around

For those who want the convenience, hiring a car is easy on Santorini. However, great care is needed as most of the roads twist and turn with many 'blind' corners and precipitous drops with no safety barriers. If you are on the island for more than one week, it may be worth hiring a car for only some of your stay as the local bus service is reliable, air-conditioned and regular in the high season (I have included bus information in a later chapter).

Obviously this mode of transport is dependant on where you are staying and how accessible your hotel/apartment is to the local bus services. Most of the supermarkets on the bus routes sell tickets and will confirm the bus times.

Taxis are plentiful and taxi-drivers are expected to speak English, but the rule sometimes doesn't seem to be followed stringently.

The main taxi stand is just below Fira square, next to the old bus depot (now used for parking bikes and mopeds). Minimum charges start at 2 € and then it depends on where you go, if you share a taxi, the driver will consider each separate party as a second tariff. The time of day, the amount of luggage and if they have to pick you up, will all be taken into account in the final charge.

To give you some idea of cost, the fare from Fira to the airport will be around 15 € and say a journey from Fira to Oia will cost between 12 and 15 € during the day.

It is always advisable to establish the fare before you get into the taxi.

Taxi tel. number: 22555

If you decide to hire a car and you are travelling with a tour company, I am sure they will offer to arrange a hire car for you. Alternatively, there is a myriad of small car hire companies on the island and my experience is that they are all of high quality and open to a little negotiation, especially at the beginning and end of the season. In Fira town you will find the majority of companies on 25th Martiou, the road that leads up the hill north from the main square.

You can budget on paying around 250 € for one week's hire of, for example, a Daewoo Matiz or equivalent, which includes air conditioning (a must especially in the high season) and power steering, with prices increasing to around 370 € for the top end specification of a jeep. However, take account of the fact that although a jeep is seen as more of a fun vehicle and will go where the lower slung 2WD cars won't, it is open to the sun (nice at first, but you can return home looking like a beetroot) and there is nowhere to lock up those valuables.

I am not being condescending, but remember to bring your driving licence with you, an obvious thing you may say, but you would be surprised how often people forget and can't hire a car! The minimum age for hiring a car is between 21 and 23 years of age, dependant on the model of car and you need to have held the licence for at least a year.

Seat belts are compulsory and 'drinking and driving' is a serious offence with harsh penalties, whether you are on two wheels or four. Police roadblocks for breath-tests, are a regular occurrence, especially in the summer months. Beware if you park illegally, the police will remove your registration plate and you will have to go and collect it from the police station, as well as of course, pay the appropriate fine. Also when travelling around the island, please be careful when parking in the villages, the roads are very narrow and the local buses weave their way through, with usually inches to spare between the bus and the houses. You will therefore be in trouble if you block the road.

I would also recommend that you take note of the advise of the car company as to which roads your particular vehicle is appropriate for. Many of the un-metalled interior roads look fine as you enter them, but they usually get progressively worse, with large potholes and sometimes with nowhere to turn around. If you don't hire a 4WD take care, or you may find yourself facing a hefty bill for any resulting damage to the car.

Fuel is readily available with modern service stations throughout the island. Prices per litre are on average just above 1 € a litre and that will include the personal service of an attendant filling the tank.

Roads are reasonably good between the resorts, but in the high season those in the towns can get very congested. One word of advise though, throughout the island there is a conspicuous lack of road signs, so make sure you obtain a copy of the hire companies road maps (I usually ask for two), or you may find yourself going round in circles.

Scooter, motorbike and Moto hire

Now we come to the hire of scooters, motorbikes and Motos. Although initially very attractive, especially to the younger visitor (as the cost is low and there are many hire companies promoting them), I have seen so many serious accidents involving this type of transport in Greece. Therefore I would recommend anyone young or old, to think again and indulge themselves in the extra cost of a car. Although all the hire companies supply crash helmets, most people you see on two wheels (or four in the case of a Moto), are dressed in shorts and T-shirts and I have seen the result of flesh contacting tarmac. Even at low speeds, the resulting injuries are enough to put anyone off the idea for life!

With regard to pedal cycles, I have included them in more detail in the chapter on 'Sports and recreation'. I have noticed a surprising number of visitors using this form of transport, but there are a lot of hills on Santorini and as I am a person who prefers a motor in front of me, I cannot quite understand the attraction, especially when you are supposed to be on holiday. However, for those that can, I have included cycle hire etc.

Tony Oswin

Bus information

Bus information

Travelling by bus within Santorini is not without its idiosyncrasies. Although there are routes to most of the main villages and beaches, bus timetables and frequencies change regularly and without notice. Also be aware that many of the public buses look like tour buses, so be careful not to make the mistake and miss your bus! The main bus depot is near the central square of Fira on the lower side road.

To give the reader some useful information, I have added the following:

Winter season frequency   : every 1- 1.5 hrs

Mid season frequency   : every hour to most areas

Summer season frequency   : every 30 minutes to most areas

The cost range for all routes is between 1 and 2.50 €.

The link between Athinios port and Fira bus depot are timed get you to your ship between 1 and 1.5 hrs prior to departure.

Bus routes

The bus to Oia goes via Firostefani and Imerovigli

The bus to Perissa goes via Karterados, Messaria, Pyrgos, Emborio, Megalochori and Perivolos.

The bus to Kamari goes via Karterados and Messaria

The bus to Vlihada goes via Karterados, Messaria, Pyrgos, Emborio, Megalochori and Perivolos.

The bus to Vourvoulos goes via Kontochori

The Airport bus goes via Karterados, Messaria and Monolithos

The bus to Akrotiri goes via Karterados, Messaria and Vothonas

Early evening is one of the busiest times on the buses as the tourists head back to their accommodation from the beaches and villages. Very soon after starting you will find that there is only standing room left on the bus, so my advice is, return a little early to miss the rush.

There are no direct buses that go from one side of the island to the other. Fira is the main bus depot and all routes go there. You therefore have to travel to the town and change buses for your onward journey to other villages or beaches.

In the middle of the high season one can find Express buses that go to Perissa & Perivolos. The up side is they skip out some of the villages and you arrive quicker. The down side is that Express buses are often cancelled although advertised.

In the high season, some bus routes operate as late as 3:00 a.m., but check first.

Bus company telephone numbers: 25404, 23821

Ferry and hydrofoil information

Ferries to Santorini

The main Greek ferry route is from the port of Piraeus and dependant on the particular route, can stop at some the following islands before arriving at Santorini:- Paros, Naxos, Sikinos, Folegranros, Anafi, Kithnos, Milos, Kimolos and Ios. High-speed ferries and hydrofoils destined for Santorini, mostly use the port of Rafina. In summer there are daily services from both these ports.

A normal ferry takes around nine hours to reach the port of Santorini from Piraeus, with the modern Blue Star Ferries taking around seven hours. Hydrofoils complete the journey in around four to five hours.

The port of Rafina is located one hour from the centre of Athens and is the nearest port to the International Airport of A.Venizelos.

Contact telephone numbers:

Port authority	: 22339
Ferry company	: 22202

Santorini to the other islands of the Aegean

Santorini has ferry connections with most of the Cyclades islands, such as Mykonos, Anafi, Amorgos, Naxos, Paros, Ios, Rhodes and Crete.

The island is also linked with the rest of the islands of the Dodecanese and with Mykonos, Syros, Samos and Thessaloniki.

Daily hydrofoils also serve the islands of Samos, Ikaria and Fourni (in the north-eastern Aegean).

Excursion boats

From the port below Fira, there are a wide range of excursions and private boat hire available. From trips around the island's coast, a visit to the volcano (page 79), private yacht hire to the other islands in the Cyclades, on-board wedding receptions, conferences and many more.

Details of these can be obtained from the companies in the port or through the many travel agents in Fira and the other resorts.

Tony Oswin

Eating and drinking

In this chapter I will first cover eating out. During the writing of this book I have meticulously sought to be unbiased and accurate with all the information I have included. However, where eating out is concerned, we have all had the disappointing experience of a poor meal in a highly recommended restaurant. Both different tastes and changing circumstances can mean that a good restaurant to one person can be an awful one to others. Therefore in this chapter, I believe it is wise and fair not to recommend any particular restaurants or tavernas on the island, but instead try to outline some basic information and useful hints.

I will say, that I have rarely had a poor meal on the island, but on that odd occasion, I have found it hard to complain when the average price of a meal is £12 - £15 per person including a glass of wine.

The tips I would pass on are as follows:

First take a good look at the taverna or restaurant in question, is it busy, does it have pleasant surroundings? A major part of eating out on holiday, is I believe, the service, surroundings and views. Remember however, that on Santorini you pay for the views, as the prices are higher in those restaurants and bars that perch on the caldera rim. Before deciding look at the menu, is it comprehensive? Don't be put off by the faded photographs of food outside the restaurant or taverna, most are like this and if you were to stand outside in the sun all day you would fade too! If you fancy fish, ask if it is fresh, by law they have to specify this. A further tip, especially outside the main resorts, look to see if the locals are eating in the restaurant, they know where to find the best food!

Service in most of the restaurants is good, if sometimes a little slow, especially when it comes to obtaining the bill, but remember you are on holiday, so relax. It is acceptable for you to ask to look at the food in the kitchen and enquire about any particular dish. You may feel a little wary at doing so, but whenever I have asked, they have been more than happy to show me around and answer any questions.

Most dishes come with French fries and/or rice and often with a small amount of salad. If you are partial to salad, it may be advisable to order an extra portion, but as you will find, they are usually large, so one will be enough for two people.

If, after your main course you do not order a pudding, many tavernas will bring some melon, mousse, or jelly 'on the house' to thank you for your custom, or you will get a small glass of Ouzo or Metaxa with the bill. It is worth keeping an eye out to see what that particular taverna's approach is.

Beware of ordering unusual liqueurs without asking the price first. On my first trip to Santorini I ordered a Glayva and almost had to take out a mortgage to pay for it!

Most tavernas and restaurants are open all day serving breakfast, lunch and dinner. For those who want a more British start to the day, (I'm afraid I'm one of those), a well-cooked and comprehensive English breakfast can be obtained at some tavernas, with only the bacon being a little different (but very tasty). The cost with juice, tea/coffee, the usual egg, bacon, sausage, beans, tomatoes and toast is between 5 and 10 €. The alternative of a continental breakfast is always available.

Lunch if you can manage it after breakfast, is usually a similar menu as evenings, but most places do snacks and salads as an alternative.

If during your visit you want something a little different from traditional Greek cuisine, there is a Chinese restaurant on the island. As it is the only one I am happy to mention it. 'China' restaurant is near the cable car in Fira. I have dined there and found the food excellent.

In the towns and larger villages, there are a number of 'fast food' outlets, where you can eat in, or buy a take away such as a rotisserie chicken, kebab, or burger meal.

A quick guide to Greek food

To help with the menu, I have outlined below a list of dishes you will usually find.

Appetisers

Mezes - A plate containing a selection of different appetisers, similar to the Spanish tapas, usually to be shared around the table. Mezes can include seafood, meats, vegetable dishes and dips.

Dolmades (or stuffed vine leaves) - vine leaves stuffed with rice and then rolled (a variation also contains minced meat). Served most often cold as an appetiser, but can also be served hot with an avgolemono sauce on top. Its origin is thought to be from Thebes about the time of Alexander the Great.

Taramosalata - Greek caviar combined with breadcrumbs, oil, onion, and lemon juice to compliment any meal as an appetiser. This is a thick pink or white puree of fish roe, dependent on the type of fish. Sometimes mashed potato is substituted for breadcrumbs.

Tzatziki - A yoghurt, cucumber and garlic dip to be served chilled on its own, or with pita or plain bread. Great on a gyro.

Keftedes - Small rissoles or fritters, often made with minced lamb, pork or veal, onion, egg and herbs and sometimes with ouzo as a moistener. Keftedes are shaped into flattened balls and usually fried. On Santorini, one local speciality you must try is their 'Tomato Keftedes'.

The following three appetisers are traditional Santorinian dishes:-

Tomato Balls

White Eggplant dip

Fava - Yellow Santorinian lentils

Main courses

Roast Lamb - Lamb prepared in the traditional Greek way with garlic inserted into the meat and cooked with bay leaves.

Roast Chicken - Both from an oven or a spit, cooked in olive oil. I personally think the rotisserie chickens are the best and taste as chicken should taste. Chicken in most restaurants on the island tends to be in fillet form, although, there are a few tavernas where you can still get a half chicken on the bone.

Moussaka - A Greek national dish, Moussaka is prepared with sliced eggplant, lean ground beef, onions, tomatoes, butter, eggs, milk, cheese and seasonings and baked in an oven.

Gyro - Thin slices of barbecued meat specially seasoned with herbs and spices, served with tomatoes and onions on pita bread, and topped with tzatziki. Best from a rotisserie.

Pastitsio - A Greek 'Lasagne' combining macaroni, minced meat, cheese and covered with béchamel sauce.

Pilafi - Fluffy rice simmered in butter, spices and rich chicken stock.

Souvlaki - Souvlaki are made from cubes of meat that have been marinated for several hours in olive oil, lemon juice & rigani, then threaded on wooden skewers and grilled or barbequed. They are usually made from beef, chicken, lamb, pork, or veal.

Stifado - Stifado is a casserole made of beef, veal or lamb in wine with pearl onions, tomatoes, herbs and spices.

Kleftico - or 'Klephtiko' is a term that refers to any kind of meat dish that is sealed and baked. The word comes from the time of the Greek revolution, when bands of Greek guerrillas, called Klephts, hid in the mountains and cooked their dinner in pits sealed with mud, so that smoke and steam would not escape and betray their position. Usually it will be Lamb Kleftico that is on the menu.

Spanakopitta - Spanakopitta is a spinach pie, about the size of a flan. These small pies are made with a spinach and feta cheese filling in filo pastry. They can also be called spanakotiropitakia. However, they are referred to as Spanakopittes in Greek bakeries and I shall do likewise.

Stamnato - Usually made with lamb (or spelt 'lamp' or 'lab' ....one reason why I love the Greeks) with potatoes in tomato and garlic sauce, baked in a traditional pot called a Lamm.

Pasta

Spaghetti Bolognese is a firm favourite on most menus (and they usually do it very well), but other pasta dishes are normally available.

Grilled meats

Grilled meat usually includes lamb chops, pork, veal and chicken, either plain or in a variety of sauces dependant on the restaurant.

Omelettes

Most tavernas offer a variety of omelettes on their menu.

Pizzas

Where pizzas are concerned there are some tavernas that specialise, having the proper ovens and expertise. So my advice would be to ask around to find the best place to go, but personally I have found most are at least equivalent in quality to the best in the UK or US.

Seafood

As with the majority of Mediterranean countries, in Greece you can find a wide variety of fresh and tasty seafood. Before ordering though, I suggest you ask if the fish is fresh and not frozen. Many restaurants and tavernas have a chilled fresh seafood cabinet near the entrance and the waiters are usually happy to confirm the range of fresh fish they have on offer.

If you fancy splashing out on a lobster dinner, those restaurants that have fresh lobster on their menu usually require 24 hrs notice; I would also ask what the price would be per person and not per kilo. If you order prawns, the average price is around 10 € and you get about six, king-sized and in their shells.

Patisseries

Melomakarona - A honey cookie sprinkled with a spice-nut mixture.

Koulouria - Also called Koulourakia - Breaded butter cookies with a light sugar glaze. Perfect with coffee.

Baklava - Nut filled, paper-thin layers of glazed filo pastry soaked in pure honey, make this the king of pastry desserts. Every country in the near-east claims baklava is its own.

Kourabiedes - Sugar covered crescent shaped cakes that melt in your mouth. They are usually served at weddings, at Christmas, and on special occasions, such as birthdays and holidays.

Diples - Honey rolls so thin and flaky that they crumble when they are bitten.

Kataifi - A delicious pastry made of shredded filo pastry rolled with nuts and honey and sprinkled with syrup. Found throughout the Mediterranean.

Loukoumades - Feathery light honey tokens or sweet fritters, deep fried to a golden brown and dipped in boiling honey. A tasty delight from ancient Greece where they were given as tokens to winners of the games at festivals.

Halva - Is a candy made from ground sesame seeds. It is an oriental originated sweet, popular in Greece.

Coffee

Greek style coffee - This is a thick, powdered coffee that is made in a brickee (or brika), which is traditionally a small brass pot with a long handle. Modern advances have given us stainless steel brikas. This is not instant coffee, and even though powdered, the coffee used does not dissolve. The grounds settle to the bottom of the cup. When you order Greek coffee, you must specify plain, sweet or medium-sweet (sketo, glyko or metrio in Greek, respectively).

You can also order Cappuccino, Expresso and other types of coffee in most restaurants. Tea is usually available, but it comes in a do-it yourself style and can taste a little odd due to the long-life milk often used. I would recommend you ask for fresh milk.

Supermarkets

The supermarkets in Fira and the villages are well provisioned for the international holidaymaker. Many brands are recognisable and if not, the supermarket staff are usually very helpful. Milk comes in cartons and although in Greek, just look out for the picture of a cow and the colour coding is the same as in the UK. As is the case in the US, what the English know as crisps are called chips in Greece and chips are known as French Fries.

If you want to eat in, supermarkets usually have a wide range of vegetables and fruit on sale, but meat, other than the basics such as cooked cold meats and bacon have to be bought from the local butcher, just ask and they will tell you where it is.

There are take-aways in the main resorts with a range of food, but if you don't have the facilities to cook meat in your accommodation, many tavernas and restaurants (if you ask nicely) will do a take-away service for main meat items such as a roast chicken.

If you want bread or pastries for later on in the day, I would advise you buy them early, as the supermarkets tend to sell out before lunchtime.

All the supermarkets sell wines and spirits, with most of the international brands of spirits being readily available on the island. The selection of lagers is also international, however, the Greek lagers, such as Mythos are in *my view* excellent. In addition to the supermarkets, there are usually dedicated off-licences in the main resorts that stock an even greater range. Prices are at least comparable with the UK and US, if not cheaper.

Shopping

Mens' clothes

As with most products on Santorini and unlike other Greek islands (Santorini has the distinction of catering for a large number of cruise liner visitors), clothes are mostly equivalent, or slightly greater in price than back in the UK or US. There is a good range of linen and cotton shirts with prices starting at around 30 €, with T-shirts, light weight trousers, shorts, summer jackets, hats and belts making up the majority of goods on offer. The variety and range for females tends to be greater, but then most men don't go on holiday to shop!

Cigarettes, sweets and newspapers

In all the towns and resorts you will notice large wooden kiosks on the pavements of the main streets. This is where in Greece you traditionally buy such items as cigarettes and tobacco, newspapers, magazines, ice-cream, drinks, sweets and snacks such as crisps. The supermarkets also sell all of these except usually newspapers.

If you smoke and from the UK, don't bother bringing any with you as they cheaper than back home, at approx. 3 € for a packet of 20 (£2.40/$4.70). You needn't shop around as the price will be the same at all the outlets. All the main international brands are available such as Marlboro, Rothmans, Superkings, Benson & Hedges, etc. As with many countries now, Greek airports as with all public buildings, are now totally smoke-free zones and on landing the rule applies until you leave the airport buildings.

For those who become homesick whilst away and want to know what new stealth taxes the government have imposed, English newspapers are available, although they may be the previous day's edition. I have personally seen on sale from the UK (although printed in Greece) The Daily Mail, The Mirror, The Sun and a couple of the main broadsheets, so you should have a good choice.

Magazines in English are more rare, but I have seen some of the main women's publications on the newsstands.

Souvenirs

Well this is a difficult subject to write about as we all have a different view of what a good souvenir is. In all the resorts, but especially in Fira, the shops are designer in nature and in many the prices reflect this. Jewellery, art and glassware shops abound, so much so you wonder how each can make a living. If you browse their windows you will see most of the fashionable and exclusive makers names from around the world. There *are* shops selling the less expensive souvenir items and I have to say the quality is generally very high. You will also find many souvenir items made from the volcanic rock of the island, but if you really get stuck, there is always the bottle of Ouzo, Metaxa or a natural bath sponge.

Personal electronic items

I have yet to survey in detail the cost of personal electronic equipment, but for the UK tourist, my initial view is that the prices are equivalent to those back home and as Greece is in the European Union, there will be no duty to pay on your return.

However, it may be a problem if the goods turn out to be faulty. If you do intend to purchase expensive items, check first that the manufacturer's guarantee will cover the item back in your country of residence.

With regard to cosmetics, fashion, hairdressers and jewellery, I will pass this section over to my partner Carol.

Cosmetics

Although Santorini is an island, as far as buying your moisturiser, body lotions, make-up etc and the all-important sunscreen you don't have to worry. Especially in the towns there is a good selection of retailers that stock most cosmetics and toiletries.

There are specialised beauty shops in Fira and most pharmacies and supermarkets sell known international products. If you cannot find your favourite brand then just ask an assistant who will be able to advise you on the Greek equivalent product. So no need to waste valuable space and weight in your suitcase, just buy all you need when you arrive.

Hairdressers

There are salons in Fira and in most of the main resorts to cater for all your follicle needs, and after a few days in the sun and sea, what better way to treat your hair, and yourself, than having a few hours relaxation and pampering, preparing for your evening out in one of the many restaurants and tavarnas.

Fashion

Thira has an extensive array of different shops to cater for every taste and age group, from fun boutiques, to designer outlets. In Fira it is best to 'shop around' first though, as depending on where the shop is situated depends on the price! Shops on the cable car route and near the caldera edge tend to be more expensive, where as if you deviate down the side alleys you will find the same items at a cheaper price, with no compromise on quality.

There is such a wide range, from bikinis and sarongs, to leather shoes and handbags, you will be spoilt for choice!

Jewellery

It seems that nearly every other shop you pass in Fira and the larger resorts sell some kind of jewellery - bangles, bracelets, rings, necklaces, earrings and much more. Designer and specialised jewellery shops are in abundance in Fira where some retailers design and manufacture their own ranges. I especially like the designs made from the local black lava stone – very different and unique, and something to treasure and keep as a memory of your visit to this beautiful island.

U.K. Customs

Regarding taking goods back home, if the goods you are carrying have had tax paid in Greece, you do not have to pay any tax or duty on them in the UK. Any alcohol or tobacco you bring in *must be* for your own use and transported by you.

'Own use' includes goods for your own consumption and gifts. If you bring in goods for resale, or for any payment, even payment in kind, they are regarded as being for a commercial purpose.

With regards to quantities allowed, you are particularly likely to be asked questions by customs officers if you have more than:

3,200 cigarettes, 200 cigars, 400 cigarillos, 3 kg tobacco, 110 litres of beer, 90 litres of wine, 10 litres of spirits, 20 litres of fortified wine (such as port or sherry).

Some goods are banned, such as plant materials and products which could contain diseases.

(All the above are correct at the time of going to press)

Money matters

Most of the banks are located around Fira's main square, but there is a branch of the National Bank in Kamari and Alpha Bank in Oia. All the banks have ATM machines, which take most debit and credit cards.

The charges for the use of your card will for the most part depend on your bank back home, so it might be wise to have a discussion with your bank/building society before you leave home and confirm the costs you will incur. If you use one of the banks on the island to exchange your US or UK currency or travellers cheques (and this may also be the case with the alternatives below), take your passport with you to confirm your identity.

Other than the banks, there are a wide range of exchange options, many hotels, shops and car hire companies will also exchange Sterling and US Dollars, but make sure you check the rate and any charges first. Again the Greeks are very honest and I have never been short-changed.....but 'better safe than sorry'.

In the banks, you may find a queue (remember life is at a slow pace in Greece), look around as there may be a ticket-machine where you can retrieve a number identifying your place in the queue.

As to the exchange rate, I certainly have found that it is generally equal or better than that found back in the UK, so if you don't want the hassle of picking up currency before you leave home, just bring cash and change it on the island (e.g. in September 2007 the exchange rate in the UK was 1.38 on the island it was 1.42).

Credit/Debit cards are accepted in many tavernas and shops on the island. However, just in case, it is advisable to carry sufficient money with you on days and evenings out. One further point regarding drawing cash out abroad via a credit card (learnt from personal experience), is that many card companies will not only charge you a relatively high exchange commission, but also an additional cash advance fee. So if you want to use your credit card abroad, I would therefore advise you check on potential charges before leaving home.

With regard to the safety of carrying money and leaving it in your room, as I have stressed before, the Greeks are extremely honest and over the last 30 years of travelling in Greece, I have never had anything stolen. On the contrary, I have accidentally left valuable items in public places, only to find them untouched hours later.... Remember though, there are not only Greeks on the island!

At the time of going to press, a helpful hint to remember is that 10 euro equals approximately £8 ($16).

The bank opening hours are Monday to Thursday, 08:00 - 14:30, Friday, 08:00 - 14:00.

However, if you are exchanging money, it is advisable to be at the bank before 14:00.

Regarding ATMs, I am afraid it is difficult to give accurate directions, as many roads do not have names. Therefore I would advise you ask for the exact location of the bank or machine locally. However, below are the number and general location of the ATMs:

Thira	- 5
Oia	- 3
Kamari	- 2
Perissa	- 2
Airport	- 2
Port	- 2

Bank phone numbers: (Prefix for Santorini - 22860)

National Bank of Greece	: 22662
Emporiki Bank	: 22534

Alpha Bank   : 23801

Agricultural Bank   : 22738

Pireus   : 25441

Eurobank   : 25739

Weather

What can you say about the weather in Greece other than as a 'Brit' I find it invariably gorgeous. To be a little more accurate, what we would call summer back in the UK usually starts in May with temperatures rising throughout the following months (see the table below). Through late April, May and early June, and then again in October, the weather can be compared to a good British summer.

The months of July and August tend to be the hottest, with average daily temperatures ranging from 82ºF (28ºC) during the day to 72ºF (22ºC) at night. The high temperatures often spark off thunderstorms in the evening, but these are not usually accompanied by rain and are more entertaining than a nuisance.

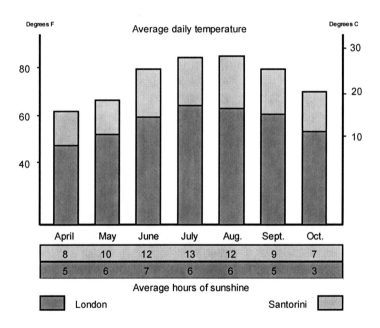

Rainfall is almost non-existent in summer, but showers can be expected between October and March.

In late April and May, the island often experiences strong breezes, but this can be of benefit, especially when the hot summer sun arrives early.

The Meltemi

The Meltemi (the Greek equivalent of the French Mistral) is a powerful wind that blows across all of the Aegean islands. It is the result of a high-pressure system over the Balkans and a low-pressure system over Turkey, creating strong northeast winds. The Meltemi occurs mainly during the summer with July and August being the worst affected months, but it can spring up occasionally in May and October. It usually starts in the early afternoon and can die out at sunset although occasionally, it will last through the night and repeat for three to six, sometimes even ten days. The winds can cause havoc with the ferry timetables and remember not to leave valuables on your balcony, or you may return to find them missing!

In October the evenings begin to cool, but that can be a blessing for those who enjoy a good nights sleep. Temperatures continue to drop through to December and in January and February the average daily temperature is 10°C to 13°C, which is more like our spring in the UK.

Bugs, biters and things

This chapter is not for the paranoid, as I have been 'true to my word' adding a definitive list of the bugs and biters on the island. However, that does not mean that any of the following are a threat to 'life and limb' and I can confirm that regarding all listed, I have never met anyone who has suffered more than the usual 'mozzy' bites or the very rare wasp sting, so with that in mind, here we go.

Mosquitoes

As with the whole of the Mediterranean there are mosquitoes on the island, but they only appear in significant numbers in July and August, but a good covering of mosquito repellent in the evenings, which is sold at all supermarkets, should generally protect you. It does seem to be dependent on the person, I rarely get bitten, whereas my partner Carol seems to attract all the little critters. Her answer is she has better quality blood!

I would advise you to use a mosquito machine in your bedroom, which can be the old plug-in heated tablet type (the tablets are still available), or the new heated liquid system. After testing the latter, they are in my view superior, one bottle of liquid should last for the whole holiday and there are no fiddly tablets to change every day.

Mosquito bites

Although there are 'over the counter' remedies available at the local pharmacies, you could try applying vinegar to the bites and you will find the itchiness will subside.

Horse Flies

Found throughout warmer climates, the Horse Fly is the largest of the fly species. Recognised by its size and a grey mottling on the back of the thorax, only the female fly bites, just prior to egg laying. If you do get bitten, make sure the fly is either swatted or gone, as they can be persistent little critters, drinking blood from the wound.

Treat any wound as you would a mosquito bite.

Wasps

A more irritating insect can be the wasp. They tend to be found in greater numbers near the populated beaches (where there is a good supply of tourist food), with the areas around towns and villages having very few if any. So it is dependant on where you are and what you are doing. However, don't worry.... the locals don't.... try to ignore them, I certainly haven't been stung and just find them irritating at times.....another answer is to buy a fly swat and see how many you can exterminate. Sorry, I apologise to the entomologists amongst you.

If you find them irritating when you eating in a restaurantl, ask the waiter for a 'burner' (smouldering Greek coffee in a container....yes it seems it has to be Greek), which is a great deterrent to the little blighters. The good news is that come sundown they all return to their nest.

Hornets

There are hornets on Santorini, but small numbers mean they are not a problem. They have a fearsome reputation for stinging and causing considerable harm, but in fact individually, they are just as harmful as a wasp or bee - no more and no less. Like most bees and wasps they usually only sting if you are blocking a flight path or are moving rapidly, however, nests should be avoided at all costs as a swarm attack can be very serious! For those that are not familiar with hornets, they have similar colouring to a wasp (being a member of the wasp family), but are about twice the size.

Ants

There are ants of course on the island and they remind me of the 'Fire Ants' of the southern states of America. Leave any food out in easy reach and you may return to find a long procession of thousands of the critters offloading it back to their nest. It can be quite an entertainment, watching them manhandle something many times their size and never giving up.

Scorpions

Scorpions…. I've never seen one on Santorini although I have occasionally seen them on other islands, but don't worry, in the most unlikely event that you would be stung, it is said to be no worse than that of a bee.

Other insects

The other insects you may observe whilst on Santorini are a wide variety of moths and butterflies, praying mantis and bumble bees.

Lizards

You will see many wall lizards whilst on Santorini, most abundantly on the hillside of Mesa Vouno. The most common species is Erhard's Wall Lizards, but don't wory they are totally harmless.

Snakes

With regard to snakes, I have only seen one that was crossing the road and I saw it too late. It is now a flat-snake! There are a number of species on the island as in all of Greece, but only one is poisonous, namely the Viper. Most vipers are nocturnal and are only sporadically observed in the daylight, when they bask or mate. It is easy to distinguish a viper from the harmless species, based on their triangular head, 'swollen' cheeks, stout body (vipers are seldom longer than one metre) and the characteristic zig-zag pattern on their back. A viper bite is not necessarily poisonous: in only about 30% of bites there is actual injection of venom, and thus a need for treatment.

The rule is if you see a snake, be on the safe-side and leave it well alone, but *please* be assured, it is extremely rare to hear of a bite. However, the precautions that can be taken are that when out walking in long grass, wear ankle length boots and do not turn large stones over, or place your hand into crevices that might be home to a snake. If you were to be the 'one in a million' and are bitten, the advice is to be safe and seek medical help straight away.

Sea Urchins

Sea urchins can be found in some areas on the island (as with most of the Mediterranean), but if you have children, a quick chat at one of the beach tavernas, or a scan for their remains on the beach will confirm whether to take precautions. If they are around the simplest solution is to wear flip-flops when entering the sea.

If you do step on one, consult a doctor or pharmacist and they will advise you on the best course of action. Don't worry though, it will usually mean nothing more serious than a little discomfort.

Here is the advice given in a medical journal:-

- Look for the signs and symptoms of a sea urchin sting: small spines embedded in the skin; a localized brownish-purple colour where the barbs made contact with the skin.
- Use sterile tweezers to remove any embedded spines.
- Control bleeding by applying direct pressure to the wound.
- Irrigate the wound with an irrigation syringe.
- Clean the wound with a disinfectant solution.
- Immerse the foot in hot water for at least 30 minutes, until pain subsides.
- Elevate the foot to control swelling.
- Dress the wound with a sterile bandage.
- Monitor for signs of infection. These signs include swelling, redness, pus, red lines radiating from the site of the wound, heat at the site of the wound, and fever.
- Seek medical advice.

Jellyfish stings

If you do experience a sting, the quickest remedy is applying urine to the affected area, so pick your holiday companions carefully!

Health

Hospitals, doctors & community clinics

Whereas we all hope that nothing untoward happens on our holidays, especially health wise, as I can personally testify it sometimes does.

My view of the islands facilities is a good one, with all but the most serious incidents catered for on the island itself. In Fira there is a Health Centre, well equipped and easy to find by following the signs in the town.

There are also private doctors in Fira and most of the resorts. Normally the surgery is near the middle of the village or resort centre and can be recognised by a red cross on the door, or on a sign in front of the building.

There are a number of pharmacies in Fira and at least one in each of the resorts. They operate on regular business hours (usually 08:00 - 13:00 and 18:00 - 24:00). One pharmacy in Fira stays open during the night and the early morning hours (check locally for details). The quality of medicines and advice is equal to that back in the UK.

For emergencies there is a twenty-four hour doctor service at the Health Centre in Fira. Alternatively there are private doctors you can visit if the need arises.

Remember, if you are a UK citizen, you should apply for an NHS distributed European Health Insurance Card (EHIC) as the previous E111 form is no longer valid. This will allow you to obtain free or reduced cost treatment abroad; this includes only treatment provided on the state scheme. The EHIC is free of charge and can be obtained in the following ways. I advise that you apply well in advance of your trip, as it can take a week or two for the card to arrive:
By internet at **www.ehic.org.uk**
By telephone on 08456062030
Or by form from the Post Office

Dental services

My own personal experience of ill health in Greece was in 2006, prior to moving to the island of Thassos to live. Only hours after arriving on the island, I was stricken by severe toothache and although I suffered for two further days (I'm a man), in the end I had to ask for help and I was recommended to a dentist in Thassos Town.

All I can say is that I was amazed at the care shown to me on my arrival and the quality of the subsequent treatment. The surgery was modern, comfortable and very well equipped and the dentist friendly, he spoke fluent English and his 'chair-side' manner was highly professional. I also found on my return to the UK, that the charges I had paid, were less than half that I would have paid at home. All in all, I have to say that if I required dental work, I would prefer to have it done in Greece, rather than back in the UK.

Contact details:

Santorini Health Centre, tel: 23123/4 – 23333

Emergency services, tel: 112

Community clinics:

First aid phone numbers:

Fira	: (22860) 22237
Emporio	: (22860) 81222
Kamari	: (22860) 31175
Oia	: (22860) 71227
Pyrgos	: (22860) 31207
Thirassia	: (22860) 23191

Dentist

Fira Dentist	: (22860) 23333

Sunburn

The most obvious advice anyone can give is 'don't get burned in the first place'! If like most, you are not used to the Mediterranean sun, take it very easy on the first few days and use plenty of high factor suntan cream. You are especially vulnerable when there is a breeze, or when you are travelling in an open top car (a point I learnt from bitter experience), as you do not feel the full extent of your skin's reaction to the sun.

If the worst does happen, my first advice is go to the local pharmacy and seek help. If this is not possible, a cold shower will initially relieve the pain, but drip dry, as using a towel will only aggravate the situation. For mild sunburn, cool compresses with equal parts of milk and water may suffice. Another remedy, recommended by many, is to spray or pat the effected areas with white or cider vinegar; this will relieve the pain and itching and hopefully give you a good night's sleep until you can visit a pharmacy.

The symptoms may also be relieved by taking asprin or ibuprofen, but do not exceed the doses specified on the label.

Stomach upset

If the worst happens, try adding a little fresh lemon juice to a Greek coffee and knock it back (so you don't taste it) and in no time at all the symptoms will ease.

Safety

Where safety is concerned, the subject falls into two categories.

First there is the safety aspect with regard to crime; one of the points that has always attracted me to Greece, especially the islands, is the lack of both property and personal crime. It does exist, or there wouldn't be police or prisons in Greece, but as far as the tourist is concerned it is rare on Santorini. What property crime does exist tends to be from the less desirable tourists and criminals from the poorer states near to Greece. If you see the police on the island they will usually be drinking coffee or chatting to colleagues. But be warned, if you do transgress the rules, the police can be quite heavy handed.

The advice is of course be careful, however, I have accidentally left expensive items in public places in the past, only to return many hours later to find them just where I left them.

With regard to valuable items and money left in your accommodation, again I have never heard of any problems. The room cleaning staff, I have met in the past, have proved totally honest and as long as you lock the windows and doors you should have no need to worry. Sadly there have been a few incidents of cars being broken into, especially when the owners leave valuables on show. So the rule is when you leave the car, put valuables in the boot and it is also worthwhile leaving the glove compartment open and empty.

In the event of a loss of a valuable item, remember that if you are insured, your insurance company will need written confirmation that the loss was reported to the local police.

The second category is safety with respect to the activities you participate in during your stay. Safety in Greece is less stringently 'policed' than in the UK or US, so when you are out and about, and especially with children, extra care should be taken. To give an example, the walls around the caldera edge in Fira are low and on the other side is a precipitous drop down into the sea, one slip could be fatal.

Being abroad you should also take extra care when driving. Although the locals are mostly good drivers, compared to say the Italians, if you are not experienced at driving on the right, mistakes can easily be made, especially on the snaking roads that abound on the island. It is a sobering sight on your travels, to look over the edge of the road to often find a drop of hundreds of metres, with at the most a small wall as a safety barrier.

As far as scooters, motorbikes and Motos are concerned, these are the most dangerous modes of transport on the island. You will see these being driven correctly with the riders mostly wearing crash helmets, however usually only with shorts and T-shirts being worn......and I have seen the damage tarmac and gravel can do to human flesh!

In Fira as in most towns, pavements are usually very narrow or non-existent, so extra care should be taken when walking in anywhere other than the pedestrianised areas.

One further point is not to trust the zebra-crossings, in Greece these mean little although the rules do give the pedestrian the 'right of way'.

Tony Oswin

Hints and tips

Currency conversion

An easy way to convert euro to pounds is to remember that 10 € is roughly £8 ($16).

Spelling

On your travels and in printed material (such as signs and menus), you will see names and places spelt in a variety of different ways. Do not be put off by the spelling, especially when you are trying to find somewhere, if it sounds the same, it probably is!

Sunbeds and parasols

If you are going to be a regular visit to the beach, rather than hire a parasol at an average of about 2.50 € a day, it may be cost-effective to buy one from one of the beachside supermarkets (between 10 and 15 €). If you don't have a car and you are put off at the thought of carrying it back to your accommodation each day, you can ask nicely at the supermarket where you purchased it and they may allow you to leave it there overnight.

The same goes with the sunbeds; a good lilo can be purchased for around 10 € (a sunbed is between 2 and 3 € a day) and gives you the added advantage of being able to use it in the sea. Many supermarkets have a compressor that they may allow you to use, so you can deflate it at the end of the day and take it back to your accommodation, or as before, ask nicely at the supermarket and they may allow you to leave it there.

Internet café

Most towns and resorts on the island have an Internet café, ask where your local one is. The cost is around 3 € an hour, which makes it a cost effective alternative to 'phoning home' and a way of retrieving your emails while you are away. But remember to take your important email addresses with you.

Mobile phones

Many mobile phone companies now offer reduced cost call packages for when you are abroad, but you will have to contact them and enquire what offers are available at the time of your trip. Also remember to get your phone unblocked for international calls before you leave home.

Telephoning

Many apartments and hotels now have phones in the room, although the cost of phoning home can be high. Alternatively many main landline providers in the UK and US as well as independent telephone prefix companies offer very low cost or even free international calls to Greece. It may therefore be cost effective to text relatives with your room telephone number and ask them to phone you. Remember Greece is 2 hours ahead of UK time and 7 hours ahead of US EDT.

Public telephones are to be found throughout the island, but remember, even in this age of mobile phones, there can be a queue of holidaymakers waiting to phone home, especially in resorts in the early evening.

To phone the UK the prefix is 0044 and you drop the first zero of the UK number, i.e. a London number that starts 020..... would translate into 0044 20.... To phone the US the code is 011 and then the full number required

To phone Greece from outside the country, the prefix is 0030 and the area prefix for Santorini is 22860.

One further option for phoning home is to use Skype, although a number of the Internet Cafes have Skype loaded, it is best to bring a headset or Skype phone with you, as not all cafes supply them. If you are familiar with Skype, you will know that phone calls home will only cost cents, compared with euros with alternative services.

Batteries

All the usual international battery sizes are available in the supermarkets at equivalent or cheaper prices than back home, but make sure you bring the battery chargers for your mobile phone, pdi, etc.

Electricity

The electricity on Santorini and throughout Greece is 220V. You can purchase the two pin adaptors at the local electricity shops. So if you do not already own one, it may be cheaper to purchase them on the island.

Water

Don't drink the tap water on Santorini. The Cyclades islands have a general problem with piped water supplies, the mineral content is very high, and since there has been no successful solution at the island's desalination plant, anything you drink should be bottled. For bathing and general washing feel free and safe to use tap water.

Water conservation is high priority and considered important on the island, since it is either expensively produced at the desalination plant, or imported from the mainland and visitors should respect this. All kiosks sell bottled water, but more reasonable prices can be found at larger supermarkets.

Toilet paper

A delicate subject, but an important one. Due to the small bore of waste pipes that are used in Greece (no....I don't know why they don't use larger ones either), it is a rule that toilet paper is not flushed, but deposited in the bin by the toilet. Although this can be a little embarrassing for some, it is better than having to call on the manager of your accommodation to help unblock the toilet. However, the bins are emptied on a regular basis and shouldn't cause a problem.

Tipping

Tipping is an awkward subject to cover as it is obviously dependant on the quality of service you have received and at your personal discretion. The service you receive on Santorini should be very good and if you take an average price for a meal for two of 30 €, a tip of 10% is not excessive and quite acceptable, being £2.40 or $4.70. The local wages are low and it may also be courteous (and prudent) to tip within these limits.

Hair dryers

Many hotels and apartments supply a hairdryer in the room. However, if important, it is advisable to check with your tour-company or hotel before leaving home.

Electric razors

Some accommodation on the island have dedicated 220V razor points in the bathrooms, but if not the adaptors sold on the island will take a twin pin razor plug.

Police

There are police stations in nearly every large village or town. You will recognize the police station by the Greek flag flying from the building and of course by the police vehicles parked outside.

On Santorini there is also a tourist police service (Touristiki Astinomia) for more holiday related problems. You will find the office of the tourist police in the same building as the island police in Fira.

The tourist police also supply information and brochures on the island and help in searching for accommodation.

Contact telephone numbers:

General Police : 22239

Tourist Police : 23172

Post

As it is a tradition with us Brits to send home the usual 'wish you were here' cards, I will cover posting on the island, but remember even if you post your cards soon after your arrival, it is highly likely you will be home before your cards!

The cost of the postcards and the stamps required for the UK/US is very low and you can purchase both in the supermarkets.

The Greek postal service is ELTA and post offices can be found in all the larger towns and are usually open from 07.30 to 14.00. Post boxes are coloured bright yellow and the post-office signs are yellow and blue.

Donkeys

Donkeys and mules in Santorini are part of the native charm of the island and can be loads of fun. During the summer the main business of the day is carting the tourists up and down the endless steep steps that connect Fira town to the small port below and to Ammoudi harbour. They are extremely adept at negotiating the steps, but they do have a tendency to go very fast and take the bends like the 'Road Runner'.

Shoes

As I have mentioned elsewhere in the book, the vast majority of roads and alleyways on Santorini are cobbled with the local volcanic stone. It is therefore advisable to wear good walking shoes, or the soles of your feet may suffer from a day's walking on these uneven surfaces.

Laundry

If your hotel or apartments don't have a laundry service, there are quality laundry services in all the main resorts. So one solution to that bulging suitcase is to bring less and let the laundry take care of the problem.

Santorini National Airport

Sadly this information will only be of interest when you are returning home. The facilities are modern and as comfortable as any departure area. Once you pass through 'passport control', there are toilets, a café supplying drinks and snacks and a small duty-free shop selling the usual cigarettes, booze and a range of those last-minute present ideas.

Tel.: 31525, 31538 or 33349

Google Earth

For those with web access, an interesting and informative site is:-

www.earth.google.com

Here you can view satellite images of Santorini (and the whole world). You will need to download the free basic version software, but it is well worth it. For quick access to satellite images of Santorini, add the following coordinates into the top left-hand corner box and press search. This will take you to Fira.

36 25 06.47N 25 25 55.19E

Weddings, Honeymoons and Romance

Weddings

Santorini has become one of the most popular destinations for both weddings and honeymoons, especially as more and more couples are deciding to arrange to have their 'special day' abroad. The spectacular and unique scenery, the fabulous weather, the breathtaking sunsets, the romantic atmosphere and the deep blue sea, attract couples from all over the world to take their vows and celebrate their new life with a honeymoon straight out of the picture books.

There are numerous companies offering to organise your wedding on Santorini, as a quick check on the internet will confirm. Whether you are planning a civil wedding, catholic wedding, orthodox wedding, or a vow renewal ceremony, there are companies that can coordinate the simplest to the most complex ceremony. Most offer either a total package, or will organise those parts that you prefer not to control yourselves. Whichever route you take, the following list contains the main issues:-

Booking the hotel for yourselves and your guests

Booking the church or venue

Organising the Greek marriage license and certificate

The translation and authentication of all documents

Hair and beauty services

Organising the reception, food and entertainment

Floral arrangements

Wedding cake

Photographer

Transportation needs

The notification of the wedding must be posted on the announcement board of the particular community at least 7 days before the service.

To give you an idea of the documents that you will have to supply (at least one month in advance) are:-

- Birth certificates of the bride and groom.

- An official document confirming that neither party is presently married. If one or both have been previously married, a divorce certificate(s) is required.

- Both the above must be in both English and Greek. The Greek consulate, in the couple's country of residence, must complete translations.

- Photocopies of the bride and grooms passports.

- Confirmation of the profession of the bride and groom.

- Full names of the parents of both the bride and groom.

- The religious denomination of both the bride and the groom.

Civil weddings can take place almost anywhere on Santorini. The most popular locations are in Fira, Firostefani and Imerovigli, all on the western side of Santorini, where the stunning scenery makes an ideal backdrop for a wedding. Some of the more unusual venues include a ceremony at a beautiful old mansion, at a traditional vineyard, or on a private veranda overlooking the caldera.

However, one thing to take into account whatever the style of wedding, is that Santorini is a very popular location and can get booked up for a year or more in advance. It is never too early to start planning and to confirm whether your preferred wedding date is available.

Please keep in mind that not all the web sites you will find through the internet regarding wedding coordination in Santorini, are from legal wedding planners. My advise would be first to check on potential companies offering their service on the internet, but then to contact the tourist office on the island, or one of the quality hotels and check which they recommend.

Whether you want an intimate ceremony with just the two of you, a small circle of close family and friends, or dance the night away with a hundred guests, Santorini will delight and amaze all.

Anniversaries and special occasions

Would you love to re-live your special wedding day by taking your vows again? Or on the contrary, was your wedding day not the way you had always dreamt of, due to weather, anxiety, rush or limited budget? If so, then Santorini is just the place to organise that special occasion and I have no doubt the memories will last forever.

Glossary of Greek words and phrases

Below, I have included a few useful words with their Greek counterparts. Although the majority of Greeks on the island speak some level of English (many putting us Brits to shame), I have found that they really appreciate our attempt to use their language, even if we make a proverbial 'pigs ear' of it!

Yes	Neh
No	Okhee
Good morning	Kalimera
Good afternoon/evening	Kalispaira
Please	Parakalo
Thank you	Efkaristo
No, thank you	Okhee efkaristo
The bill please	To logargiasmo parakalo, or simply make a gesture in the air as though you were signing your name…..it works!
Hello/Goodbye (singular/informal)	Yiassou
Hello/Goodbye (plural/formal)	Yiassas
How much	Poso Kani
Coffee	Kafé
Tea	Tsai
OK	Endaksi

Where is	Pooh eeneh
Do you speak English	Meelahteh ahnggleekah
I don't understand	Dhehn kahtahlahvehno
Can I have	Boro nah ehkho
Can we have	Boroomeh nah ehkhoomeh
I'd like	Thah eethehlah
Tomorrow	Avrio
Today	Seemera
Toilets	To tooalettes
Wine	Krassi
Good	Kahloss
Bad	Kahkoss
Bank	Trapeza
Police	Astinomeea
Doctor	Yatdros
Now	Tora
What is the time	Ti ora ine
Cheers	Yammas
Sorry/excuse me	Signomee

Greek timeline

Date	Event
2700 - 1450 B.C.	The period of the Minoan civilisation. The term Minoan was 'coined' by Arthur Evans at the beginning of the 20th century. He was the archaeologist who excavated Knossos on Crete. He believed he had found the palace of the fabled King Minos…hence Minoan civilisation
1450 - 1100	The Mycenaeans are the dominant civilisation on mainland Greece and in the Aegean
1100 - 800	The Greek 'Dark Ages'
776	First Olympic Games
circa 750	The start of early Greek culture. Homer 'writes' the epics the 'Iliad' and the 'Odyssey'
508	Athens becomes a democratic state
490 & 480	Athenians defeat the Persians at the battles of Marathon (490 B.C.) and Salamis (480 B.C.)
472-410	Athens flourishes. Most of the famous Greek plays are written during this period
460-370	Hippocrates, the 'father' of medicine
404	Sparta defeats Athens at the end of the Peloponnesian Wars (431 - 404)
338	King Philip of Macedonia takes control of Greece
336	Kind Philip is murdered, most likely by Alexander and his mother
336-323	Alexander the Great, son of King Philip, conquers most of the known world, as far as India
146	Rome conquers Greece and subjugates it as part of the Roman Empire

Early Roman timeline

Date	Event
509 B.C.	Traditional founding of the Roman Republic
396	Romans capture Estruscan city of Veii
390	Rome is sacked by Gauls after its army is slaughtered at the river Allia
275	The Pharos lighthouse at Alexandria is finished
264-241	First Punic War
218-201	Second Punic War
216	At Cannae, Rome suffers its worst defeat to the Carthagian Hannibal
202	Hannibal is decisively defeated at Zama
200-196	Second Macedonian war
192-188	War with Antiochus III
171-167	Third Macedonian war
149-146	Third Punic War
146	City of Carthage is destroyed
133	Tiberius Gracchus introduces novel reforms including land grants to the poor and food distribution; he is murdered
123	Gaius Gracchus, brother of Tiberius is also murdered after initiating reforms along the same lines
107	Gaius Marius is elected consul; begins major reforms of army
88	Rome grants citizenship to all free adult males in Italy
82	Sulla becomes dictator

77	Senate chooses Pompey to put down Sertorius's rebellious army in Spain
73	Uprising of slaves led by Spartacus
71	Crassus and Pompey defeat Spartacus
60	Pompey, Crassus and Caesar form the First Triumvirate
59	Caesar elected consul
58-51	Gallic Wars conquest of Gaul by Julius Caesar
53	Crassus dies at the battle of Carrhae
49	Caesar defeats Pompey at Ilerda in Spain. Crosses Rubicon river; initiating civil war
48	At battle of Pharsalus Caesar defeats Pompey
46	Caesar becomes dictator
44	Brutus, Cassius and other senators assassinate Caesar
43	Octavian, Antony, and Lepidus form Second Triumvirate
42	Antony and Octavian defeat Brutus and Cassius at the battle of Philippi; destroying the last republican army
40	The Roman Senate makes Herod the Great King of Judea
33	Civil war between the armies of Octavian and Antony
31	Octavian crushes the naval forces of Antony and Cleopatra at the battle of Actium
27 B.C.	Octavian takes the title of Imperator Caesar Augustus; the empire begins

Imperial Rome timeline

Date	Event
27-14 A.D.	Reign of Augustus as Emperor
9 A.D.	Three Roman legions annihilated by Germanic tribes at the Battle of the Teutoburg Forest
14-37	Reign of Tiberius
37-41	Reign of Caligula
41	The mad emperor Caligula is stabbed to death
41-54	Reign of Claudius
43	Claudius orders the invasion of Britain
54-68	Reign of Nero
64	Great fire in Rome. Persecution of Christians
66	Beginning of Jewish revolt
69	'The Year of The Four Emperors'
69-79	Reign of Vespasian
70	The city of Jerusalem is virtually wiped out by Titus
79-81	Reign of Titus
79	Eruption of Mt. Vesuvius; the twin cities of Pompeii and Herculaneum are buried in ash
80	Colosseum (Flavian Amphitheatre) opens
81-96	Reign of Domitian
85	Agricola's campaigns in Britain end
98-117	Reign of Trajan
101-106	Trajan conquers Dacia. Arabia becomes a province

112-113	Trajan's Forum and Column dedicated
115-117	Jewish revolt
132-135	Bar Cochba's revolt; final Diaspora of the Jews. Hadrian's Villa built at Tivoli. Hadrian's Wall built in Britain
142	Wall of Antoninus Pius built north of Hadrian's Wall
165-167	Rome suffers from severe plague
168-175	Marcus Aurelius campaigns in German wars
208-211	Severus campaigns in Britain. Arch of Septimius Severus erected
211 - 217	Caracalla is Roman Emperor
284-305	Diocletian's Reign
306-337	Constantine's Reign
312	The Emperor Constantine converts to Christianity. The Edict of Milan grants legal rights to Christians
325	The Council of Nicea – to agree the future of the Christian Church
330	Constantine declares Constantinople capital of a Christian Empire
circa 372	The Huns conquer the Ostrogoths
378	Battle of Adrianople, eastern Emperor Valens is killed by the Goths
379-395	Reign of Theodosius
395	Death of Theodosius I, final division into an Eastern and a Western Empire
396-398	The Visigoths ravage Greece
402	Ravenna becomes the capital of the western empire

410	Rome is sacked by the Visigoths
418	Visigoths settle in Aquitaine with capital at Toulouse
429	The Vandals cross from Spain to Africa
436	Last Roman troops leave Britain
441	The Huns defeat the Romans at Naissus
circa 450	Beginning of Anglo-Saxon settlements in Britain
451	Aetius defeats Attila at the Catalaunian Plain
453	Council of Chalcedon: Constantinople wins ecclesiastical supremacy over Alexandria
455	The Vandals sack Rome
476	Romulus Augustulus - last emperor of the west is forced from his throne by the Germanic chieftain Odoacer, who is proclaimed King of Italy
532-537	Justinian builds the Church of Hagia Sophia
533-534	Re-conquest of North Africa from the Vandals
535-555	Re-conquest of Italy from the Goths
541-543	Great Plague
548	Death of the Empress Theodora
568	The Lombards invade Italy
681	The First Bulgarian Empire is formed
690's	Muslims conquer Byzantine North Africa
717-718	Muslims lay siege to Constantinople
1453	Fall of Byzantine Empire when Turks capture Constantinople

Map of the archaeological site of Akrotiri

A. North Mill
B. North Magazines
C. House of the Ladies
D. West House
E. House of the Lilies
F. House of the Anchor
G. House of the Antelope
   and the Boxing Children
H. Xeste Three
I. South Building

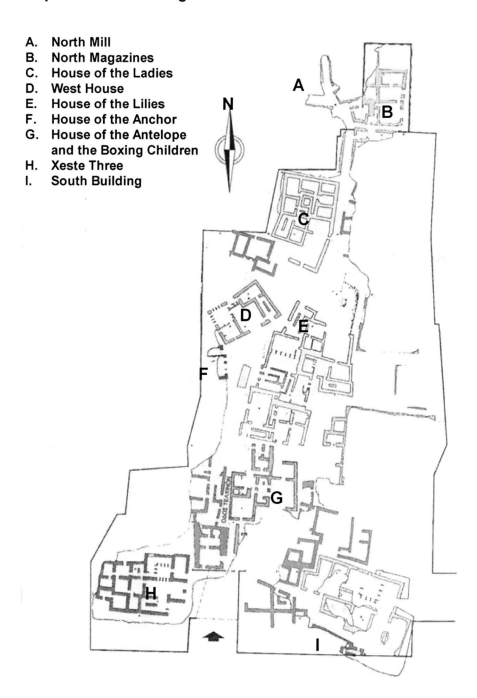

Acknowledgements and web sites of interest:

I would like to thank the following for their help in the writing of this book.

The people of Santorini
Athina Dimitropoulou, Amerisa Suites Hotel
Wikipedia
gWebsolutions
Walter I. Friedrich, Dept. of Earth Sciences, University of Aarhus

I have also included web pages that you may find of interest before your visit to the island.

www.greeka.com
www.paleologosco.com/
www.amerisa.gr
www.china-santorini.gr

2009

January 2009

Su	M	Tu	W	Th	F	Sa
				1	2	3
4	5	6	7	8	9	10
11	12	13	14	15	16	17
18	19	20	21	22	23	24
25	26	27	28	29	30	31

February 2009

Su	M	Tu	W	Th	F	Sa
1	2	3	4	5	6	7
8	9	10	11	12	13	14
15	16	17	18	19	20	21
22	23	24	25	26	27	28

March 2009

Su	M	Tu	W	Th	F	Sa
1	2	3	4	5	6	7
8	9	10	11	12	13	14
15	16	17	18	19	20	21
22	23	24	25	26	27	28
29	30	31				

April 2009

S	M	T	W	Th	F	Sa
			1	2	3	4
5	6	7	8	9	10	11
12	13	14	15	16	17	18
19	20	21	22	23	24	25
26	27	28	29	30		

May 2009

S	M	T	W	Th	F	Sa
					1	2
3	4	5	6	7	8	9
10	11	12	13	14	15	16
17	18	19	20	21	22	23
24	25	26	27	28	29	30
31						

June 2009

Su	M	Tu	W	Th	F	Sa
	1	2	3	4	5	6
7	8	9	10	11	12	13
14	15	16	17	18	19	20
21	22	23	24	25	26	27
28	29	30				

July 2009

Su	M	Tu	W	Th	F	Sa
			1	2	3	4
5	6	7	8	9	10	11
12	13	14	15	16	17	18
19	20	21	22	23	24	25
26	27	28	29	30	31	

August 2009

Su	M	Tu	W	Th	F	Sa
						1
2	3	4	5	6	7	8
9	10	11	12	13	14	15
16	17	18	19	20	21	22
23	24	25	26	27	28	29
30	31					

September 2009

Su	M	Tu	W	Th	F	Sa
		1	2	3	4	5
6	7	8	9	10	11	12
13	14	15	16	17	18	19
20	21	22	23	24	25	26
27	28	29	30			

October 2009

Su	M	Tu	W	Th	F	Sa
				1	2	3
4	5	6	7	8	9	10
11	12	13	14	15	16	17
18	19	20	21	22	23	24
25	26	27	28	29	30	31

November 2009

Su	M	Tu	W	Th	F	Sa
1	2	3	4	5	6	7
8	9	10	11	12	13	14
15	16	17	18	19	20	21
22	23	24	25	26	27	28
29	30					

December 2009

Su	M	Tu	W	Th	F	Sa
		1	2	3	4	5
6	7	8	9	10	11	12
13	14	15	16	17	18	19
20	21	22	23	24	25	26
27	28	29	30	31		

Vertex42.com

Notepad

Notepad

Printed in the United States
217545BV00006B/1/P